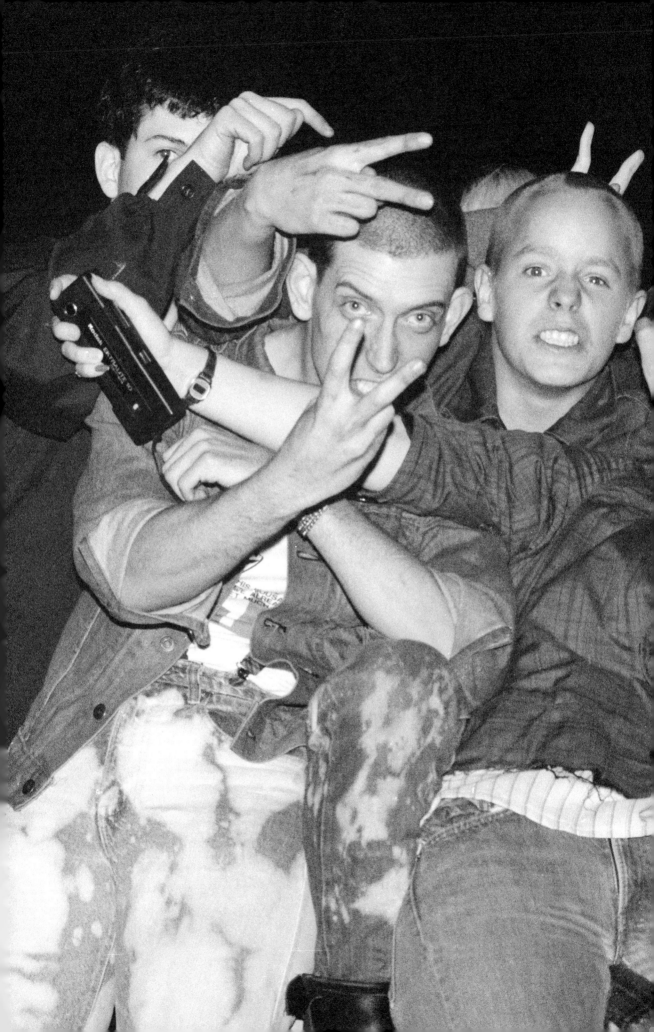

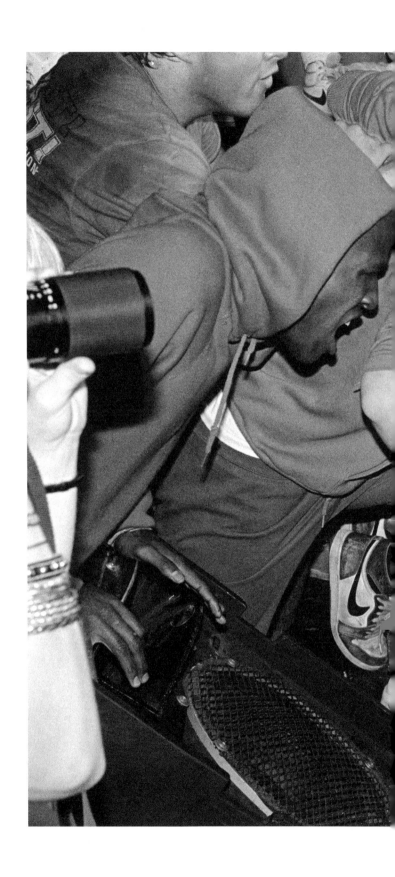

Radio Silence / A Selected Visual History of American Hardcore Music
Copyright© 2008 Nathan Nedorostek and Anthony Pappalardo
The copyright of all photographs, illustrations, records, T-shirts, and fanzine images that appears within
the pages of *Radio Silence* remains with their respective authors /publishers.

radiosilencebook.com

Produced and edited by Nathan Nedorostek and Anthony Pappalardo
Editorial direction - Anthony Pappalardo
Design direction - Nathan Nedorostek
MTV Press - Jacob Hoye, Lollion Chong
Production - Mike Troast
Scanning - Tom Bolger, Jackie Anderson
Copy editor - Fiorella Valdesolo
Legal - Dave Stein
Intern - Jacob Pastrovich

The authors would like to thank Matt Owens and Mark Owens for their support and guidance.

First published in the United States of America in 2008 by MTV Press, A Division of
MTV Networks 1515 Broadway, New York, New York 10036. mtv.com

Distributed by powerHouse Books 37 Main Street, Brooklyn, New York 11201. powerhousebooks.com

FIRST EDITION 2008
PRINTED AND BOUND IN SINGAPORE
ISBN: 978-1-57687-472-1
Library of Congress Control Number: 1025408350654

000.001 [cover] Hand painted leather jacket, circa 1987. Illustration by Gavin Ogelsby, courtesy of Casey Jones, photograph
by Nathan Nedorostek; **001.002: Bad Brains** at Viceroy Park, Charlotte North Carolina, January 16, 1982. Photograph by
Rusty Moore; **002.003: Negative Approach** at The Clubhouse, Detroit, 1982. Photograph by Davo Scheich; **004.004: SSD**
at The Channel, Boston, Massachusetts, March 1983. Photograph by Gail Rush *This gig was just after **SSD** and **DYS** members
had come from filming the **Misfits** 'Braineaters' video in Durgen Park. Lots of brains, blood, and innards had been thrown around.
Springa had a pigs head he got at a butchers near the shoot. He brought it on stage for 'Police Beat' where it was thrown around
and torn apart.* — GAIL RUSH; **005.005: Chain of Strength** at Spanky's Cafe, Riverside, California, 1989. Photograph by
Dave Sine; **006.006: Sick of It All** at The Pyramid, New York, New York, 1989. Photograph and hand coloring by Theresa
Kelliher; **008.007:** Lyle Preslar, Wendel Blow, and Sab Grey outside the 9:30 Club, May 1982. Photograph by Rusty Moore;
010.008: Crippled Youth at the Rathskeller, Boston, Massachusetts, May 11, 1986. Photograph by JJ Gonson

Radio Silence /A Selected Visual History of American Hardcore Music

Nathan Nedorostek and Anthony Pappalardo

Intro BUST! by <u>Nathan Nedorostek</u>

I was 9 when I first came into contact with hardcore at a skateboard shop in suburban Connecticut. I saw a kid wearing a T-shirt with the words "Minor Threat" crudely scrawled on the front with a black marker. I had no idea what Minor Threat was but there was a subconscious quality to the artwork that struck me. That first encounter motivated me to figure out what Minor Threat actually was, but, most importantly it inspired me to go and make my own T-shirt.

Black markers are still an easy way to make you own T-shirt, but now the tools available are more professional and readily available. However, convenience is no substitute for style and originality. Good artwork is a reflection of the time in which it was made. A dialogue is created between the author and viewer based on a mutual understanding of the time period. Today our drag-and-drop culture facilitates more creative dialogue but at the same time disconnects us from the personal relationships that are integral to the growth of a subculture. This is the antithesis of hardcore. While compiling *Radio Silence*, Anthony and I quickly realized that the challenge was not in finding content, but in communicating to everyone that we did not just want scans of old flyers and anonymous jpegs. We wanted to meet people and understand who they are as individuals so we could better tell their stories. Hardcore cultivates a very personal relationship with everyone that invests themselves in it and that had to come through in the book.

The importance of the work we collected for *Radio Silence* is defined by the circumstances and motivations of the creators. The conveniences we take for granted today did not exist. The artwork was a product of whatever means of reproduction that was available, and that greatly effected how the message was communicated. The results were sometimes unpredictable but always sincere.

Anthony and I made a conscious effort to document this body of work as objectively as possible in order to preserve the context in which it was made, and, more importantly, the people who made it. Where ever possible, we collected comments and images from the original authors that help to paint the picture of the time in which it was made. Hardcore is more than just music; it is a combination of records, T-shirts, fanzines, flyers, live shows, and folklore peppered with learning-by-doing hands-on experience. This broad spectrum could literally fill volumes. This is a selected collection that represents one perspective of hardcore up to 1994. We encourage you to fill in the gaps with your own story.

Author's note

Detailed credits accompany every image in the book along with a six digit catalog number. For instance, David Bett's original type lock-up for New York City Hardcore: *The Way It Is* compilation 12", is catalog number 086.098. The first three digits are the page number, this record is on page 086. The last three digits are the image number as it appears in the sequence of the book, this record is 098 in the sequence of the book.

page number   catalog number

086.098 [opposite below]
Original type lock-up **New York City Hardcore:** *The Way It Is* compilation 12", Revelation Records, 1988; Typography by David Bett

Instinct and Attitude/
The Art of Necessity

Anthony Pappalardo

"Hardcore was a reaction to punk. Americans have a history of messing up the program, we did it in 1776, we've done that all throughout history, we're good at messing stuff up and making it better. Hardcore was looking at punk, we made it faster, tougher, harder and made it unique and American, it's really an American genre of punk." Dave Smalley

In the late 1960s, two bands hailing from Michigan laid the groundwork for punk. The Motor City Five and The Stooges aren't the center ring of punk's tree, but they stand as the most recognizable starting point. Both bands' revved-up version of the blues garnered attention, major label deals, and devout fans, but the landscape wasn't yet ripe for a revolution. Ultimately, a shitload of heroin and the typical cast of clueless suits caused both bands to end prematurely. Nevertheless, the energy these pioneers channeled into their live performances connected with fans, making them part of the experience, not merely spectators. Iggy Pop's well-documented stage antics with The Stooges and the MC5's political roots and interactive live shows became key ingredients for the next wave.

New York City's CBGB club was the church for the new gospel in the mid-1970s. There the Ramones began speeding through punk anthems alongside an eclectic cast of acts exploring unfamiliar sounds including Blondie, Talking Heads and Television. The attitude in New York was infectious but it was a trip across the pond that set punk's wheels in motion. Credit Malcolm McLaren for being drawn to the punk styles he saw in New York City, specifically Richard Hell's self-styled ripped shirts, which he redesigned and sold at his boutique SEX in London. Soon enough his brand had spokesmen; a band he named the Sex Pistols. The Ramones weren't commercially successful stateside, but their speedy approach was embraced in the UK and ignited a crop of British bands including the Damned, Sex Pistols and the Clash, all of whom John Peel would eventually debut on his BBC radio show.

The punk phenomenon gripped Los Angeles in the late-1970s as well. Unlike many hardcore and punk scenes to form in the years to follow, Los Angeles had a diverse mix, with women and openly homosexual men being active contributors to the scene. It was a stark contrast to the macho, male-dominated stereotype often associated with hardcore. Art and presentation commingled with angst in their version of punk.

Pat Garrett and David Brown created Dangerhouse records and released a string of singles that documented their budding scene and created a blueprint for American punk record labels. British punk bands, many signed to major labels, were privy to top producers and expensive recording studios. Dangerhouse didn't have the funding to compete with major labels so they compensated with ingenuity. They found cheap production alternatives that looked professional. Records were packaged in plastic bag sleeves with printed sheets of paper trimmed into covers. Recording budgets were small, but the attention to the production kept them from sounding amateur. *Class War* by the Dils and *We've Got the Neutron Bomb* by the Weirdos became anthems that were

018.009 [opposite]
The Boston Crew in
'The Combat Zone' Boston,
Massachusetts, 1982;
Photograph by Gail Rush
*My daughter, Christine Elise
McCarthy, was part of The Boston
Crew, and she asked me to photograph
them together, not just individual
bands but as a crew. I was shooting
out front of a strip club called The
Naked I when a cop came by to see
what was going on with this huge
crew of teenage boys. He laughed
when he saw what was happening.
He said 'Move along. People won't
come in or out of here with a
camera at the door.'*
— GAIL RUSH

019.010 [below]
Weirdos *We Got The Neutron Bomb*
7", Dangerhouse Records, 1978

reacting to the social climate in the United States. The *Yes L.A.* compilation was another masterstroke. The one-sided screen-printed 12" record boasted songs from Los Angeles bands including the Bags and X, along with a group that hugely influenced the sound that became hardcore, the Germs. Beneath the distorted guitars and shouted vocals of many punk bands were crude pop songs. The Germs' sound was rooted in chaos and actually got harsher and faster as they progressed.

Wearing swastikas for shock value, disrespecting the Royal Family, and displaying a disdain for anything considered "normal" was punk's calling card. Punk was appropriating icons from fetish shops. Punk was bands named the Buzzcocks and the Vibrators. It was the Clash taking equal parts roots reggae and the Ramones. Looks were manic but manicured, deliberately crafted to destroy and annoy. Punk's roots were in New York streets, the art scene in Los Angeles, and London fashion, places totally foreign to kids in suburban America. As romantic as it was to be a starving artist living like shit in New York City most kids just fucking hated their parents and liked to light fires in the woods. As punk migrated to the suburbs the sound and attitude changed.

> *Punk claimed to speak for the neglected constituency of white lumpen youth, but did so typically in the stilted language of glam and glitter rock - 'rendering' working classness metaphorically in chains and hollow cheeks, 'dirty' clothing and rough and ready diction. Resorting to parody, the blank generation, described itself in bondage through an assortment of darkly comic signifiers - straps and chains, strait jackets and rigid postures. Despite its proletarian accents, punk's rhetoric was steeped in irony.*[01]

The anxiety, angst and apathy of America's youth wasn't being communicated by chart toppers like Wings or The Bee Gees. As the corner was being turned into the 1980s, punk's edge had been dulled by a safer, marketable strain called new wave. Punk's forefathers were becoming the caricatures they sought to dethrone. Taang Records founder Curtis Casella experienced the change. "Our favorite punk bands departed from the original sound. The Clash started playing arenas, the Ramones went totally 1950s with *End of the Century*, Generation X broke up, and Billy Idol did 'Mony Mony.' It was about making money and a hit record, and it worked for most of the bands so we sought out harder aggressive music. It was coming from everywhere: Black Flag in L.A., Dead Kennedys from San Francisco, Minor Threat, Misfits and SSD from the East Coast. By 1981-1982 all the bands had records out, this became the new punk."[02]

Something snapped in American culture; kids who loved the speed and *fuck you* attitude of punk took hold of its spirit, got rid of the "live fast, die young" bullshit and made a revision: hardcore. It wasn't a direct *fuck you* to punk's aesthetic and sound, hardcore was moving too fast to give a shit. The 1980s were pock-marked with recession, inflation, and unemployment. With an actor elected as President and a defense initiative named after the popular movie *Star Wars*, the decade was as dire as it was absurd. Cocaine was huge, AIDS surfaced as a global epidemic, and the suburbs were really fucking boring. Hardcore's direct and naïve sound stood out as the most honest commentary put to music at the time.

Hard rock, glam, and metal gave kids something to pound their fist to but nothing to sink their teeth into. Rock 'n' roll nihilism was about following your cock and ego around until it was stroked and coddled. Punk and hardcore were a middle finger to arena rock jokers. New York City artist Sean Taggart adds, "I loved the heaviness of AC/DC and Black Sabbath, but Bad Brains seemed more relevant to me. Reagan Youth were talking about shit I could understand. I didn't know a damn thing about 'stuffin' some muffin'. I was sixteen and hadn't been laid."[03]

Punk leveled the playing field and made being in a real band something tangible and attractive to any kid. Hardcore embraced that ideal and localized it. The blueprint was there, the seeds were planted, and the book was open. Making music and putting out records was no longer smoke and mirrors and could be done with little or no budget. As punk's spawn, hardcore was moving like a stray bullet, conscious of where it came from, but unsure of where it was headed. The dividing line was in the delivery—less pretense, less melody, more aggression. This urgency seeped its way from the music into the look of hardcore. There wasn't time to mold your liberty spikes or shine your Dr. Martens. It was jeans and T-shirts, shaved heads, and worn-out sneakers. The Jamie Reid ransom note aesthetic gave way to black-and-white photographs of packed shows accompanied by bold typography boasting slogans such as: *The Kids Will Have Their Say*, and *Nervous Breakdown*.

The attitude and speed of British punk influenced this new branch that was forming spontaneously around the U.S.. "*Love Song* by the Damned is absolutely the template

seed for hardcore," adds Chain of Strength drummer Chris Bratton. "The beat and bass line crystallized hardcore."[04]

Sonically, hardcore was built around faster tempos, and power versus melody. Black Flag, the Middle Class, and Bad Brains were among the first to etch this tempo onto vinyl. The focus was on output, with songs clocking in at less than a minute, devoid of a chorus or bridge. The lyrics weren't sharp jabs at Parliament, they were simple and direct messages with easily recited chants. There was no agenda or plan, just drive.

Hardcore was an outlet to vent about parents, teachers, government officials, and peers; from the guy calling you a "faggot" for having a Mohawk, to the politician reassuring you about how great things were while scaring the shit out of you with the threat of nuclear war. The overindulgence of the 1980s gave birth to a new enemy for middle class kids to rally against. There was a vile breed of slim, trim, perfectly groomed plastics developing coke habits while flaunting their status and parent's bank accounts. "Cool kids" dressed like pirates, and partied to Duran Duran soundtracks. They crashed borrowed Corvettes while buzzed on pills from mom's medicine cabinet. This arrogant and materialistic stereotype, depicted best in Bret Easton Ellis' novel *Less Than Zero*, was the perfect target.

Hardcore's goal wasn't turning a profit or garnering fame, it was simply to keep going. This self-sustained economy catered to kids. Shows were a few dollars, and records were sold for a slight profit, if any at all. You didn't wait for a touring band to conveniently stop by your town and sell you a concert shirt; most bands didn't tour let alone have merchandise. If you wanted to show your allegiance to a band you took a marker and scrawled their name on anything you could wear. The breakthrough format was the 7" single. Most people called them 45s, the A-side bearing the hit single and the B-side boasting a throwaway track. They were packaged simply in dust jackets, most without picture sleeves. When slowed down to 33⅓ RPM these records held almost seven minutes per side, perfect for a genre known for short songs. Covers were created on photocopiers and layouts were done by hand. The music was

020.011 [opposite]
Black Flag *Nervous Breakdown* 7";
SST records, 1978

021.012 [above]
Dead Kennedys at Emerson
College, Boston, Massachusetts, 1982;
Photograph by Philin Phlash

interactive. Most records came with lyric sheets so you could sing along, plus stickers or ads for other records. Sold for only two or three dollars, the medium provided bands an affordable way to release their own material to fans surviving on single digit allowances.

A show packed with fucked up kids and fast music sometimes meant violence and instability, but there was always an underlying communal theme that permeated even the thickest skull. Everyone participated in one form or another; kids started record labels, borrowed equipment, photographed shows, found venues, designed record covers, published 'zines and did it all at a faster pace than the aging corporate rock machine.

Bands pressing their own records in the late 1970s gave way to the next logical step, forming their own labels. Jello Biafra created Alternative Tentacles in San Francisco, California to release records from his politically-charged band Dead Kennedys. In Long Beach, California Greg Ginn renamed his ham radio electronics business, Solid State Tuners, SST to release his band Black Flag's debut single. Ian MacKaye and Jeff Nelson used the six hundred dollars left over from their recently defunct band Teen Idles to release a posthumous single and launch Dischord records in Washington, D.C.. Dischord exclusively released music from bands based in D.C., which unified their scene and inspired others to do the same. Tesco Vee's fanzine-turned-record label, Touch and Go (later handed off to Corey Rusk) became the face of the Midwest. Boston-based bands collectively released their records under the XClaim moniker. While most high school graphic arts students were cropping photos for the yearbook, hardcore kids were distributing their wares globally. A cohesion of attitude and style developed within each scene creating a greater diversity among the whole. Each label was a testament to its scene's ambition. Channels and paths for bands that shunned the cut-throat world of rock 'n' roll were being created daily with their own rules.

In the pre-Internet world the lines of communication were mainly word of mouth, independent record stores, late night college radio, and fanzines. If you were lucky enough to live close to a thriving scene you could get most information firsthand. "You didn't have any national resource so you made your own." says Dischord records co-founder Ian MacKaye. "Every scene had its own version, its own style. If you wanted to be a punk rock kid and go to shows the bands you saw were usually local bands. Your scene would develop a certain type of rhythm and approach." [05]

Pressed records in limited runs and lacking mainstream distribution made finding hardcore records an undertaking. Mail ordering records became commonplace, and fanzines acted both as a source of information about the scene and as illustrated catalogs that wired you in no matter where you were. Fanzine editor Tony Rettman details the importance of these publications. "The most indispensable fanzine of the time was Northern California's *Maximumrocknroll*. With a press run somewhere in the thousands, nationwide distribution, and a monthly street date, it was the most consistent of all the hardcore publications. I treated *Maximumrocknroll* more or less as a buying guide, since most stores didn't stock many of these little pieces of hardcore vinyl. The only way to get them in your backwards burg was to stuff an envelope with well-concealed cash and wait by the mailbox for the goods to arrive." [06]

The best way to spread the word about your band was playing shows, anywhere and everywhere, and letting people experience your energy. Armed with a relentless tour ethic and motto dubbed the "Blasting Concept," Black Flag defined hardcore. They would play anywhere, to any crowd, their live shows frequently teetering on or becoming riots. Often times do-it-yourself became a convenient excuse for doing a shitty job or lacking professionalism. Do-it-yourself by Black Flag's standard meant giving 100% every time they took the stage, no matter how many people were watching [see 066.070]. Black Flag's drive to be the heaviest, tightest, and most productive band was an inspiration to every scene they touched. Along with Canada's DOA, they proved that hardcore bands could tour nationwide, opening the channels for everyone. Big Boys member Tim Kerr explains the impact: "Black Flag and DOA busted the door open to lots of places to play, and scenes that you may not have been aware of through *Flipside* or *Maximumrocknroll*. Some scenes started up because Black Flag and DOA had come through. Bands started coming and not only bringing their music but glimpses into their scene." [07]

Meanwhile, the mainstream media ignored hardcore. What attention it received was typically limited to a sensationalized piece about the dangers of slam dancing, or a parental warning about this rising "anti-establishment movement." Even in New York City, hardcore was rarely covered anywhere outside of the scene itself. Gorilla Biscuits' founder Walter Schreifels says "*The Village Voice,* as alternative and leftist as it was, never mentioned CBGB in the late 1980s. It was this full-blown youth culture

Pay to Cum!

Bad Brains

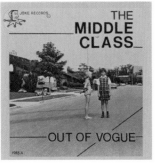

THE MIDDLE CLASS

OUT OF VOGUE

that was totally ignored. People came from New Jersey, Long Island, and Westchester, and mixed with real kids from the Lower East Side." [08]

Just as they had done with punk a decade earlier, major labels saw an opportunity to cash in on hardcore following the success of grunge. Bands with a punk pedigree proved to be a commodity. The hunt for the new Seattle was on, and labels started sniffing underground music's ass looking for the next "Smells Like Teen Spirit." When the ink dried, they ended up with multi-platinum *Dookie*, a few frustrating Offspring songs that still haunt us, and package tours full of future tax write-offs.

The affordable technology becoming available in the early 1990s was attractive to an underground music scene steeped in the do-it-yourself mind-set. Aided by home computers, fanzines morphed into magazines trying to turn a profit with jacked-up ad rates and faux-journalism. Handshake recording contracts gave way to lengthy manifestos full of legal jargon. The pseudo professionalism was as laughable as our floppy haircuts and striped Gap shirts. Over a decade of productivity created a touring circuit, viable independent labels and hundreds of bands. Splinter genres of hardcore like crust, emo, straight edge, and riot grrrl were drawing crowds without mixing bills.

The bold blue circle featured on the Germs' 1979 debut *GI* stands both as one of the first hardcore icons and a prophetic symbol of the cyclical nature of hardcore itself. When one wave becomes bloated and strained, barely resembling itself, another is teeming with urgency, itching to shoot its fucking mouth off. Some factions in the early 1990s brought things back to basements and VFW halls, away from overstuffed clubs where fights were frequent. Other bands embraced the stronger channels as an opportunity to take their music to the next level without watering it down to Sunset Strip pop-metal.

It's quickly forgotten by older generations that their salad days are always going to be another generation's check-out time. The critical ears of yesterday's fans forget hardcore is the sum of many parts. What you don't get in those two-minute anthems is the importance of those parts, and what they mean when the engine is humming along. No matter how much you romanticize your "remember whens," stomachs didn't growl harder in your heyday. Hardcore is living right now and it's just as vital as the first note of *Pay to Cum* to its audience. Bands are forming and kids are plotting. The world sucks, hearts are being broken, and parents are still as fucked up as their children. America's youth is just as bored and fed up as you were at 15.

Without platinum record certifications or a true mainstream moment hardcore still expanded into a global youth culture. It's impossible to count the labels, bands, records, demos, websites... a few decades ago anyone involved could rattle the list off in a few minutes. In the wake of 9/11 the entertainment industry rushed to provide us with the nostalgia we needed to help deal with the new America. We eagerly put ourselves in a state of retro culture where every "new" idea was a direct throwback or reference to our world before the terrorism that grips the rest of the world touched us. There was an instant romanticism for everything pre-9/11 from the old New York jangle of the Strokes to clip shows recapping every sliver of pop culture. With our pockets stuffed with disposable income aided by sketchy home loans and stimulus checks we consumed and fetishized every part of our past. Remix culture was born on September 12th, 2001. Hardcore's close alignment with nostalgia and tribute lead to any band that once was taking the stage again to give us our old world sugar fix.

As we dive into a new Republican-aided recession with oil costing fifty lives a barrel the landscape is changing rapidly. File sharing ultimately doesn't hurt Lars Ulrich, especially when you pay over a hundred bucks to see him try to play the drums, but it's taken away CD sales that become gas money for the working class band. If it will cost you three hundred bucks in gas to get from Boston to D.C., can you afford to be a hardcore band? If the door is more than eight dollars you're a fucking rock star and recording contracts are drying up so maybe it's time to dust the 4-track off. The sound and look will always change, each generation bringing their world to the table, but the sting of feeling fucked up, vulnerable, or just fed up will continue to draw the out-of-step to a haven called hardcore.

01 Hebdige, Dick. *Subculture: The Meaning of Style,* 1979, London: Methuen.
02 Interview with Curtis Casella, April 6, 2008
03 Interview with Sean Taggart, January 19, 2008
04 Interview with Chris Bratton, March 18, 2008
05 Interview with Ian Mackaye, March 7, 2008
06 Excerpt from an untitled fanzine essay by Tony Rettman, December 10, 2007
07 Interview with Tim Kerr, March 13, 2008
08 Interview with Walter Schreifels, November 25, 2008

All you hippies better start to face reality / All your far fetched dreams of anarchy / Better start to see things the way they are, cause the way things are going they won't be goin' far / World peace can't be done / It just can't exist / World peace can't be done / Anarchy's a mess.

Cro-Mags "World Peace"

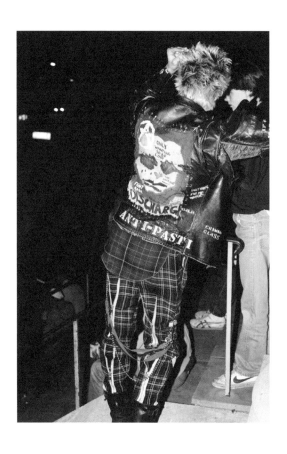

026.016 [left]
John Falls outside the
Wilson Center, summer 1982;
Photograph by Rusty Moore

026.017 [below]
Dance floor at the Wilson
Center, summer 1982;
Photograph by Rusty Moore

027.018 [opposite]
Hand-painted leather jacket, 1986;
Illustration by Gavin Ogelsby,
courtesy of Casey Jones

"In 1981 there was a moment where the whole scene started to have its own life, it was like being in the middle of a flood: you're hanging out on the ground and then all of a sudden this water comes and you're lifted up and everything is just carried away and you're with it. It's going faster than you can keep up with… You would fold 7" single sleeves, wondering how a thousand of these would sell, and then they sell out and you're back folding more. The interaction with people when you went to shows was a different type of energy than what you get from looking at websites and through e-mail on a computer. You had people interested in what you and your friends were doing, and very soon the interest became exponential and strangers were interested in what you were doing. At that point in time, I had never experienced anything like it before. The expansion of interest in the whole scene had spread by word of mouth, and the concept of that fast-growing interest was something I sometimes couldn't comprehend."
Cynthia Connolly

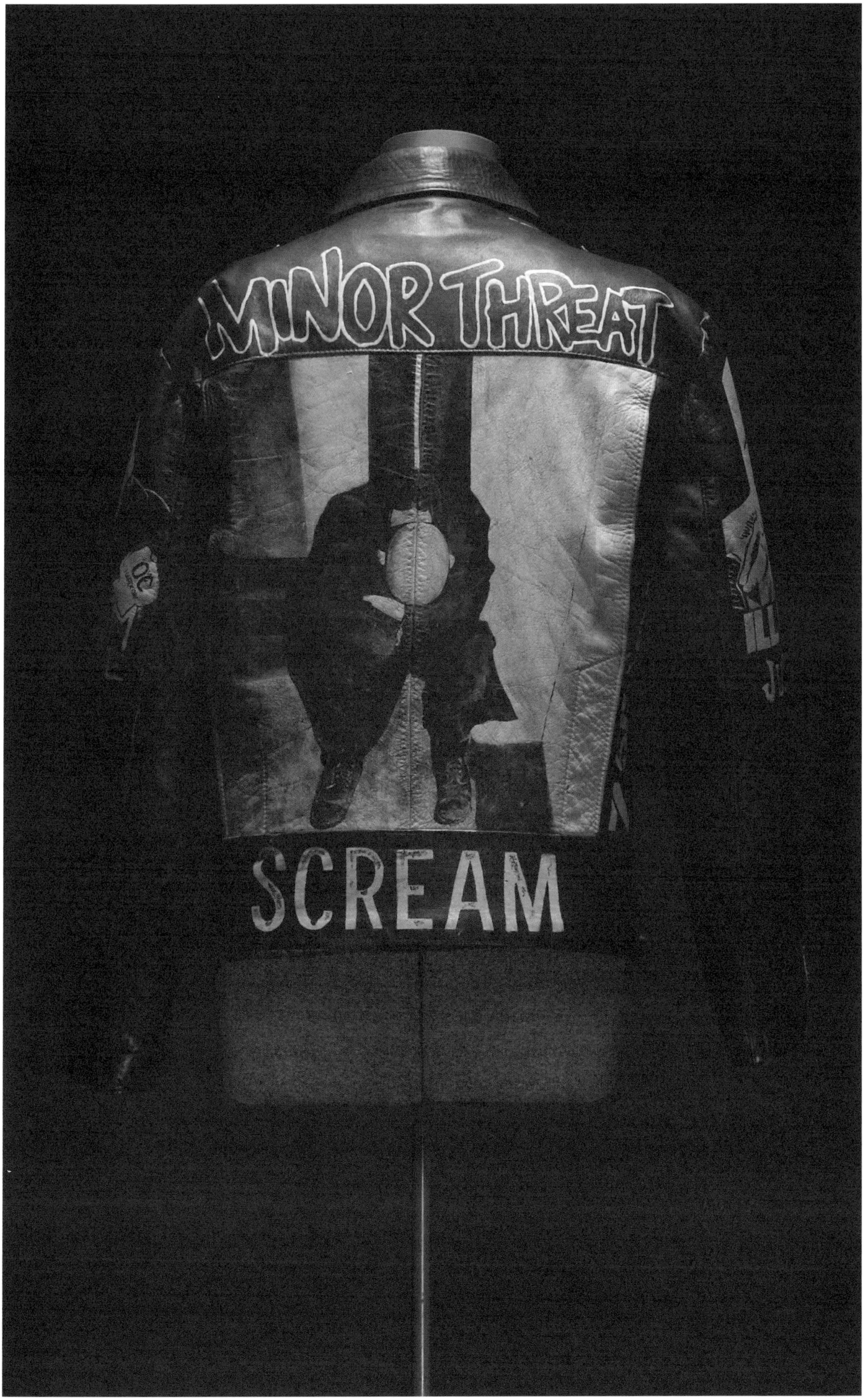
MINOR THREAT
SCREAM

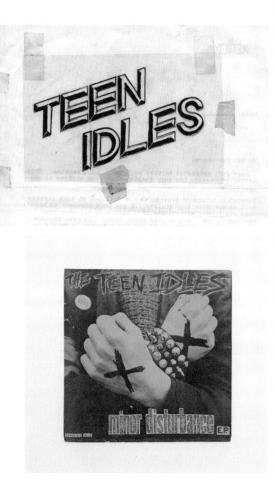

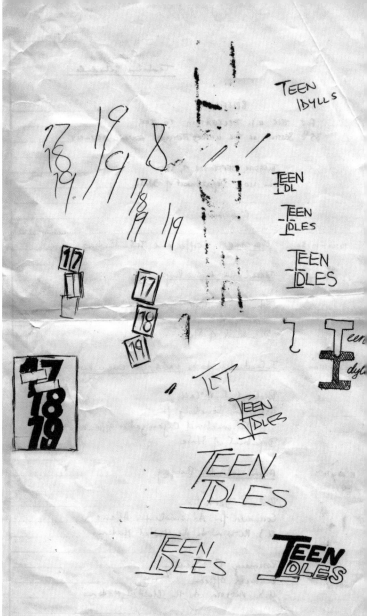

"The Teen Idles graphics were still cut and paste, and Xerox. I discovered press type and Letraset later on. They were rub on letters, you'd line them up one letter at a time. It was incredibly laborious. The record plant called us when we sent the artwork in, because they wanted to make sure that it wasn't a joke. They thought the paste up was just there as a basis for them to set the type properly. I was offended and said 'No that's the actual artwork.'"

Jeff Nelson

"My music, and Boston hardcore in particular, always had to have a fist, it had to have that power. DYS and Dag Nasty had a fist to it. I remember going to see AC/DC and Yngwie Malmsteen was opening up for them He was a technically amazing guitar player but it was just lacking that power, then AC/DC played and there was that fist."

Dave Smalley

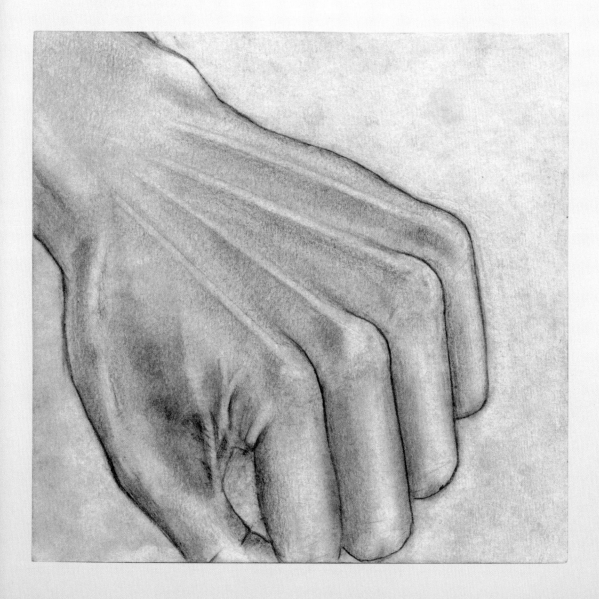

030.025, 031.026 [previous spread]
Teen Idles Army jacket, c. 1980;
Jacket courtesy of <u>Jeff Nelson</u>,
photograph by <u>Erik Lee Snyder</u>

032.027 [this page, clockwise]
Flex Your Head 12" [Blurred Head
cover]; Dischord Records, 1982

032.028
Flex Your Head 12" [XXX cover]
original printer mechanical;
Dischord Records, 1982

032.029
Flex Your Head 12" [Wheat cover]
<u>Jeff Nelson</u> photocopy experiments;
Dischord Records, 1982

032.030
Flex Your Head 12" [Violin cover];
Dischord Records, 1982

033.031 [opposite]
Void artwork for the *Flex Your
Head* 12" insert; Dischord Records,
1982; Illustration by <u>Bubba Dupree</u>

"D.C. introduced sophistication. It wasn't the punk band arguing with their parents anymore, the music was more dynamic and there was a feeling that the presentation was controlled and deliberate rather than impulsive. They didn't rely on the crazy live photographs, they took pictures in warehouses and fields, so each band had a specific look and feel."

Gavin Ogelsby

"The concept of the black sheep [on the cover of *Out of Step*] was that it was the child's naïve sort of happy-go-lucky interpretation [of the watercolor sheep]. Originally I colored it more in an adult way, so then I went in and tried to make it look childlike again.

The headshots on the back cover were shot in the Dischord dining room. It was really cold because no one could afford heat and we were holding those photo flood lights that Ian found in the trash. [We shot] black and white film but Jeff took them to a color processing place, so they came out really weird."

Cynthia Connolly

"Dave Eight showed up with a Minor Threat record and said 'You won't believe this... I think it's illegal.' Every song had some un-deleted expletive. It sounded more powerful than all the stuff we had heard up to that point, but still had a slightly more mature sense of song structure. It really stood out from the rest of the music we had heard. Once we focused in from 'hardcore' to 'harDCore,' we pretty much shut all the other stuff out."

Jason Farrell

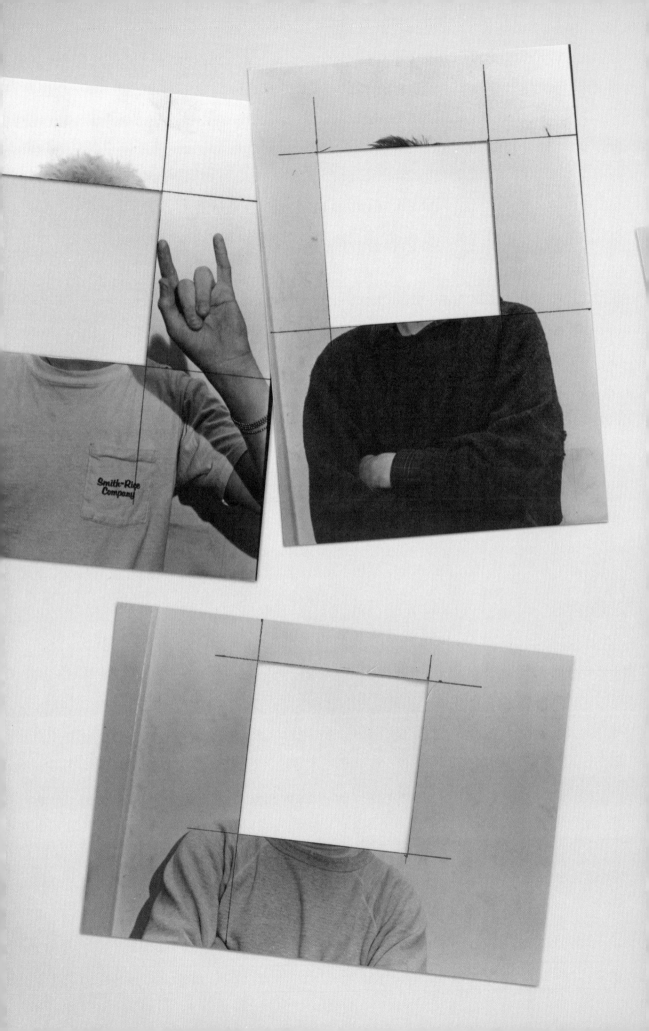

036.036 [previous, clockwise]
Portrait of Brian Baker, Jeff Nelson,
Lyle Preslar, Ian MacKaye,
and Steve Hansgen, at Dischord
House, Washington, D.C., 1983;
Photograph by Cynthia Connolly
Jeff Nelson saved these photo
scraps while redesigning the back
cover of the **Minor Threat** *Out of
Step* 12" for its second pressing.

038.037 [right]
Minor Threat at the Patrick
Henry Elementary School,
Arlington, Virginia, May 15th, 1982;
Photograph by Rusty Moore

040.038 [following spread]
Dag Nasty *Can I Say*, cassette
original printer mechanical;
Dischord Records, 1986;
Design by Jeff Nelson

"Inner Ear Studios owner Don Zientara's daughters attended Patrick Henry Elementary School, and Don was put in charge of entertainment at the school fair. We played along with a country band, I think, alternating back and forth after several songs. Ian changed all the swear words in our songs to clean them up a bit, like 'you're full of poop.' Many of the kids covered their ears. The best part was when we played during a game of 'cake walk,' while we played some furious 30-second song, little kids ran like mad around a circle of chairs. Then when we suddenly stopped playing they all scrambled and sat in the chair closest to them to see who won a cake. After playing this show, we had to leave immediately to drive four hours to New York City, where we played with Double-O and Bad Brains at Club 57."

Jeff Nelson

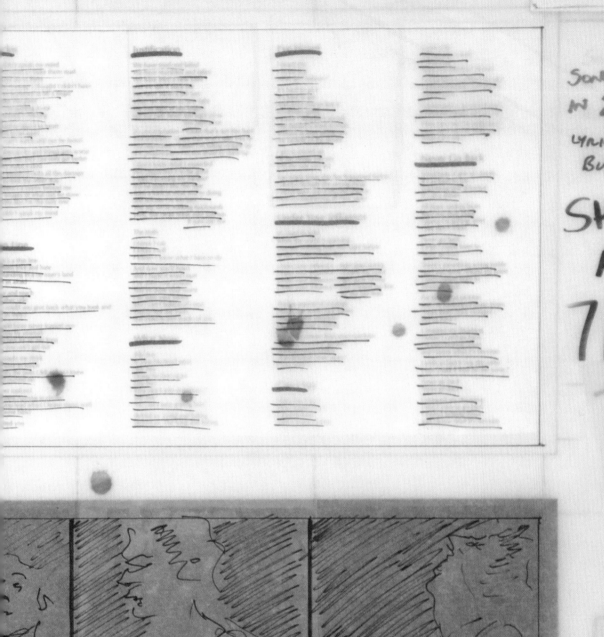

EMBRACE

DOVE

LUNCH MEAT

BEEFEATER

79 BAD BRAINS
HR Gary Earl Daryl
Voc. Guitar Drums Bass

SLINKIES
Mark Ian Jeff Ge...
Voc. Bass Drums Gu...

TEEN IDLES
Nathan Ian Jeff G...
Voc. Bass Drums

80 EXTORTS
Lyle Simon Wendel Mike H.
Voc. Drums, Bass Guitar

STATE OF ALERT
Henry Simon Wendel Mike H.
Voc. Drums Bass Guitar

MINOR THREA...
Ian Jeff Lyle Br...
Voc. Drums Guitar Ba...

81 ASSAULT AND BATTERY
Brian G. Steve Rob Mike
Guitar Voc. Bass Drums

[to Snakes]

[to Black Flag]

S.O.A. 2
Henry Ivor Wendel Mike H.
Voc. Drums Bass Guitar

[to ...

ARTIFICIAL PEACE
Steve Pete Rob Mike
Voc. Guitar Bass Drums

FAITH
Alec Mike H. Ivor Chris B.
Voc. Guitar Drums Bass

[to G.I.]

82 from Red C & Enzymes]

SKEWBALD / GRAND...
Ian Jeff Eddie Je...
Voc. Drums Guitar

MARGINAL MAN
Steve Pete Andre Kenny Mike
Voc. Guitar Bass Guitar Bass

MINOR THREA...
Ian Jeff Lyle B...
Voc. Drums Guitar

PEER PRESSURE
Tom B. Toni Danny David B.
Voc. Bass Drums Guitar

FAITH 2
Alec Eddie Ivor Chris B.
Voc. Guitar D...s Bass

83 BLACKWATCH
Danny Jen R. Breton Norman
Voc. Bass Guitar Drums

MINOR THREA...
Ian Jeff Lyle Brian
Voc. Drums Guitar Bass

GRAND MAL (WÜRM BABY)
Joey Don Linda Malcolm
Voc. bass Drums Guitar

[to Rites of Spring]

SOCIAL SUICIDE
Brian H. Danny Joey Ben A.
Voc. Drums Bass Guitar

MINOR THREA...
Ian Jeff Lyle
Voc. Drums Guitar

[to Madhouse]

[from Mob]

[from Extorts & Slinkies]

Eric T...
Voc. Guitar

84 H.R.
HR Earl Judah Dave J. Dave B
Voc. Drums Bass Guitar Guitar

KING FACE
Mark Pat Toast Simon
Voc. Guitar Bass Drums

[from BMD]

H.R. 2
HR Earl Judah Kenny Dave B.
Voc. Drums Bass Guitar Guitar

KING FACE 2
Mark Colin Simon
Voc/bass Drums Guitar

Ray Lyle
Voc. Guita...

H.R. 3
HR Earl Judah Teco Mark
Voc. Drums Bass Guitar Guitar

KING FACE 3
Mark Larry Pat
Voc/Bass Drums Guitar

85 BAD BRAINS 2
HR Gary Earl Daryl
Voc. Guitar Drums Bass

THE BELLS OF
Alec Peter Lawrence Blue
Voc. Drums Guitar Bass

Shaw...
Voc.

GRAND MAL
Joey Don Mark Linda
Voc. Bass Guitar Drums

EMBRACE
Ian Mike H. Chris...
Voc. Guitar Bass

D.C. FAMILY TRE

photos by Al

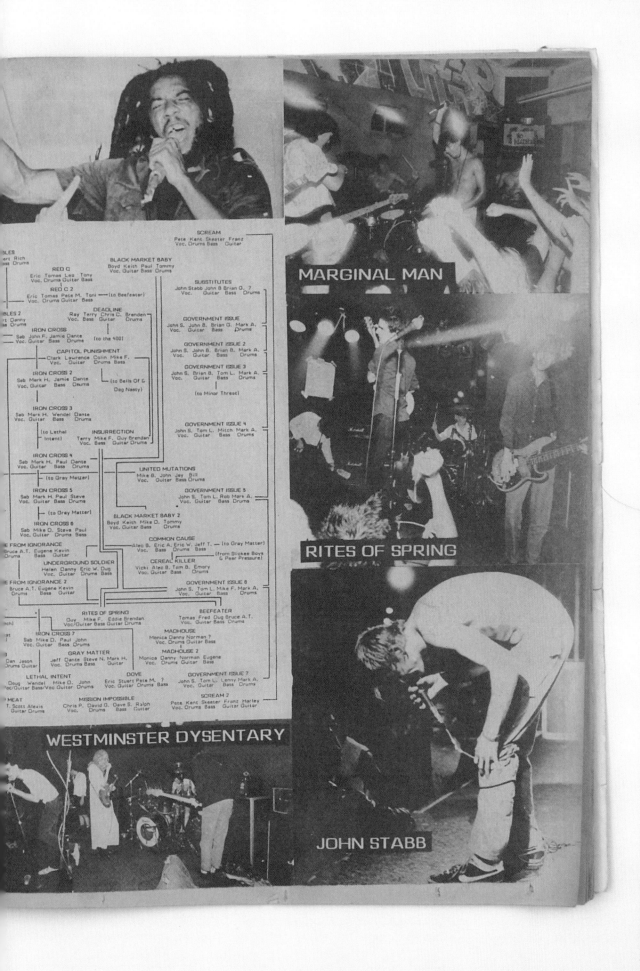

MARGINAL MAN

RITES OF SPRING

JOHN STABB

WESTMINSTER DYSENTARY

SCREAM
Pete Kent Skeeter Franz
Voc. Drums Bass Guitar

...BLES
...ert Rich
...ass Drums

RED C
Eric Tomas Leo Tony
Voc. Drums Guitar Bass

BLACK MARKET BABY
Boyd Keith Paul Tommy
Voc. Guitar Bass Drums

SUBSTITUTES
John Stabb John B Brian G. ?
Voc. Guitar Bass Drums

RED C 2
Eric Tomas Pete M. Toni — (to Beefeater)
Voc. Drums Guitar Bass

...BLES 2
...rt Danny
...ass Drums

DEADLINE
Ray Terry Chris C. Brenden
Voc. Bass Guitar Drums

GOVERNMENT ISSUE
John S. John B. Brian G. Mark A.
Voc. Guitar Bass Drums

IRON CROSS
Sab John F. Jamie Dante
Voc. Guitar Bass Drums   [to the 400]

GOVERNMENT ISSUE 2
John S. John B. Brian B. Mark A.
Voc. Guitar Bass Drums

CAPITOL PUNISHMENT
Clark Lawrence Colin Mike F.
Voc. Guitar Drums Bass

GOVERNMENT ISSUE 3
John S. Brian B. Tom L. Mark A.
Voc. Guitar Bass Drums

IRON CROSS 2
Sab Mark H. Jamie Dante
Voc. Guitar Bass Drums   (to Bells Of G
Dag Nasty)

[to Minor Threat]

IRON CROSS 3
Sab Mark H. Wendel Dante
Voc. Guitar Bass Drums

GOVERNMENT ISSUE 4
John S. Tom L. Mitch Mark A.
Voc. Guitar Bass Drums

(to Lethal
Intent)

INSURRECTION
Terry Mike F. Guy Brendan
Voc. Bass Guitar Drums

IRON CROSS 4
Sab Mark H. Paul Dante
Voc. Guitar Bass Drums

UNITED MUTATIONS
Mike B. John Jay Bill
Voc. Guitar Bass Drums

(to Gray Matter)

GOVERNMENT ISSUE 5
John S. Tom L. Rob Mark A.
Voc. Guitar Bass Drums

IRON CROSS 5
Sab Mark H. Paul Steve
Voc. Guitar Bass Drums

(to Gray Matter)

BLACK MARKET BABY 2
Boyd Keith Mike O. Tommy
Voc. Guitar Bass Drums

IRON CROSS 6
Sab Mike O. Steve Paul
Voc. Guitar Bass Drums

COMMON CAUSE
Alec B. Eric A. Eric W. Jeff T. — (to Gray Matter)
Voc. Bass Guitar Drums

...E FROM IGNORANCE
...ruce A.T. Eugene Kevin
...Drums Bass Guitar

(from Stickee Boys
& Peer Pressure)

UNDERGROUND SOLDIER
Helen Danny Eric W. Dug
Voc. Guitar Drums Bass

CEREAL KILLER
Vicki Alec B. Tom B. Emory
Voc. Guitar Bass Drums

...E FROM IGNORANCE 2
...Bruce A.T. Eugene Kevin
...Drums Bass Guitar

GOVERNMENT ISSUE 6
John S. Tom L. Mike F. Mark A.
Voc. Guitar Bass Drums

RITES OF SPRING
Guy Mike F. Eddie Brendan
Voc/Guitar Bass Guitar Drums

BEEFEATER
Tomas Fred Dug Bruce A.T.
Voc. Guitar Bass Drums

IRON CROSS 7
Sab Mike O. Paul John
Voc. Guitar Bass Drums

MADHOUSE
Monica Danny Norman ?
Voc. Drums Guitar Bass

GRAY MATTER
Jeff Dante Steve N. Mark H.
Voc. Guitar Drums Bass

MADHOUSE 2
Monica Danny Norman Eugene
Voc. Drums Guitar Bass

...Dan Jason
...Drums Guitar

LETHAL INTENT
Doug Wendel Mike O. John
Voc/Guitar Bass/Voc Guitar Drums

DOVE
Eric Stuart Pete M. ?
Voc. Guitar Drums Bass

GOVERNMENT ISSUE 7
John S. Tom L. Lenny Mark A.
Voc. Guitar Bass Drums

...MEAT
...T. Scott Alexis
...Guitar Drums

MISSION IMPOSSIBLE
Chris P. David G. Dave S. Ralph
Voc. Drums Bass Guitar

SCREAM 2
Pete Kent Skeeter Franz Harley
Voc. Drums Bass Guitar Guitar

042.039 [previous spread]
Flipside fanzine #47, 1985;
Published by Al Flipside

044.040 [above]
Rites of Spring at Food for
Thought, July 29, 1984; Photograph
by Cynthia Connolly

045.041 [opposite above]
Rites of Spring *End on End* 12";
Dischord Records, 1985

045.042 [opposite below]
Embrace *s/t* 12"; Dischord
Records, 1987

"When I saw Rites of Spring for the first time, it was clear something else was going on. One-by-one our friends decided they needed to announce to each other that they would no longer be slam-dancing. It no longer made much sense at these smaller, more intimate shows, nor was it welcomed. New bands were influenced by Rites of Spring's sound over, say, Government Issue's, and named themselves with prepositional phrases."

Jason Farrell

"The first thing I noticed when I saw Rites of Spring was that you had to have beads to be down with this new thing. If you had black beads you were really down and secondly you had to have the Hanes pocket T-shirt. I was really into the band but was confused and conflicted because I had that other side that just wanted to go crazy and let out aggression. The line was drawn for sure. They felt like we shouldn't be dancing and letting out energy, and my thought was 'Why are you telling me what to do? I thought we were punk-rockers.'"

Shawn Brown

"I encourage bands to do their own art or ask someone to help them make their art because I want a connection to the people making the music."

Ian MacKaye

"Embrace is a band that is timeless. They didn't play straight power chords, they had this totally unique and artistic approach. Another one was Marginal Man. Their guitar player Kenny had played these great Rikk Agnew sounding parts. They had these amazing tempo fluxes and incredible melodies."

Joe D. Foster

"With Swiz we were always trying to stay true to what we felt hardcore was, which was playing hard and fast, riding skateboards, and just rocking out. I was definitely one who really wanted to try to evoke that strange feeling that you get sometimes when you're listening to Black Flag. They were one band that would make me feel weird. There is such a mood and atmosphere that their music created that I still can't describe, and that was something I was always trying to tap into."

Shawn Brown

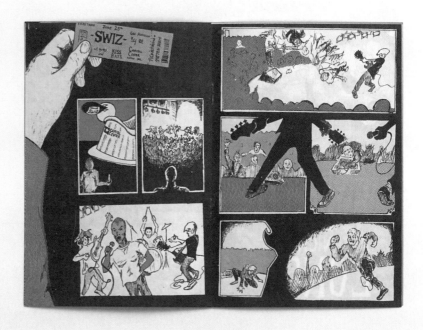

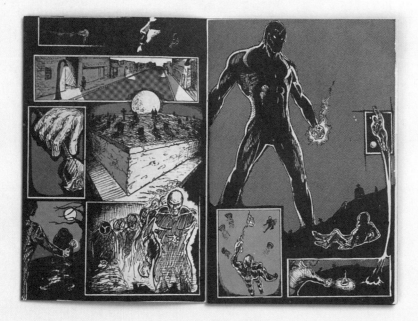

046.043 [above left]
046.044 [above right]
046.045 [left]
Swiz *Down* comic book insert; Hellfire #2, 1987; Illustration by Jason Farrell

047.046 [opposite above]
Swiz at Gilman Street, Berkeley, California, summer 1989; Photograph by Dave Sine

047.047 [opposite below]
Swiz *Down* 7"; Hellfire #2, 1987; Photograph by Becky Maury, design by Jason Farrell,

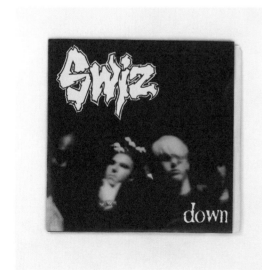

"The sleeve was a rip off of *Salad Days*. The comic book and lyric sheet were printed at my old high school. I suggested the title *Down* because every song had that word in the lyrics. Lawrence from Bells Of… got really mad because *Down* was the name of one of his songs. He probably would have let that slide, but we used a photo of me jumping off a cliff, an idea he had 'reserved' for his record when it came out some day. To top it off, I stole the opening guitar lick for *Lie* from a Bells Of… song called *Amounts* so I was pretty much on his shit list for ever. In my defense he told me how he had stolen that riff from an abandoned Rites of Spring song. He changed it slightly, moved it up the neck, and called it his own, I just moved it back down and added a country trill.

I had drawn a series of flyers featuring this superhero dude, mostly because Shawn worked in a comic book store. So we figured why not throw in a comic book with our first record. Not the clearest story line, but the gist was supposed to be a kid laying a rose on the grave of hardcore, thereby resurrecting its sleeping ghost, who then shoots him two tickets to a Swiz show where they rocked all… night… long…

The scary logo was a style of lettering I had been messing around with for about a year. The way it became our logo was fairly random. I came to one practice with Swiz written all over my Peavy cabinet, all these different ways. For one, I stole the lighting bolt *S* from KISS to make the *S* and *Z*, then put a little *wi* between. The scary lettering won hands down, but Alex asked me to remove the *X* dotting the *i* and replace it with a regular [but still scary] dot so no one mistook us for edge."

Jason Farrell

MORTICIA,
    THANKS FOR THE PHOTOS. THAT PIC OF
ME + NECROS WILL BE ON INNER SLEEVE OF
LP. WHICH IS COMING OUT ON SLASH IN FEB. WILL
SEND YOU A FREE COPY. ALSO ENCLOSED IS
A FREE T-SHIRT, WILL BE AT 930 CLUB
SUN FEB. 28 ALSO AT MARBLE BAR IN BALT.
SAT. FEB. 27. COULD I GET A 5"x4" OF
EACH OF THE PHOTOS BELOW. IF SO WRITE
        + LET ME KNOW,
          HOW MUCH THEY
          WILL BE. OH YEA,
        NECROS ARE PLAYING
        W/US IN D.C.

"The Misfits didn't play often in the late 1970s. They were totally mysterious. I remember hearing that they would only play once a year on Halloween, and that they were all crippled. Then when I first saw them it was weird because the performance was really 'comic book,' but in a good way, it was like a schtick. I wasn't prepared for that. I take things really seriously so I thought they were going to be these really fucked up creepy guys. The midwest scene really rescued the Misfits. They had a huge following there and I think that inspired the band to get out and play."

Ian MacKaye

"Right after hearing the Necros I wrote to the contact address on the record. Barry
Henssler sent me a letter back with photos and stickers. He turned me onto [a lot
of] other bands. That's when I realized [hardcore] was a network."

ROA

"The Freezer Theater was a long skinny room with hard surfaces on the floor and
walls. The sound was horrible. Those eleven egg cartons were [top right below]
the most effort anyone ever made to try and make The Freezer sound better.

The worst sounding band to play at The Freezer: Misfits. They just turned
their amps up louder. It was so bad. I stood outside the club when they played,
and I'm a big Misfits fan. The best sounding band to play at The Freezer: Minor
Threat. They were the only band who bothered to have a sound check and make
adjustments for the space."

Davo Scheich

052.056
Negative Approach at the Freezer
Theater, Detroit, Michigan, 1982;
Photograph by Davo Scheich

"We saved and borrowed to pay for *Brotherhood*. We didn't have any budget, and we had to get this record done. If there is angst it was because we were punks angry at everything, but there's also angst because there was tension. It was our first time in the studio, first time making a record, you don't know what you're doing, the engineer is asking you to do a track over and you don't know what you did wrong. That all came out in the album. We knew *Brotherhood* was going to be the title of that album because it defined our friendships, and our fights. Once there was a swarm of jocks who were getting out of the local high school while we were all hanging out on Newbury Street. Jon Anastas had this little motor scooter that he couldn't get going, and he's frantically trying to kick the thing while hundreds of jocks are pouring out ready to kill us. They grabbed Springa but he was a master at escaping a tight spot. Spray-painting the names of the bands on walls, going out to eat together at diners in Kenmore Square with everyone's jaws dropping in horror, fear, or admiration: All that… that made me realize that the bond, almost ganglike was special. To this day I understand why people join a gang and what they get out of it, I have a better understanding than most social workers because I've been in one."

Dave Smalley

"Who can forget Jon Anastas with eyeliner on the back of that second DYS 12"? That cover is indeed a classic piece of artwork but it's also the cover of a Black Sabbath *Greatest Hits* record as well. One interesting side note is that they did meet with Michael Alago, the Elektra A&R whiz who signed Metallica and later White Zombie at Geffen. One DYS gig that specifically stands out was one snowy night at a VFW hall in Malden, Massachusetts where both DYS and the FU's proclaimed it was going to be their 'last hardcore show ever.' Come to think of it, what a slap in the face to everyone who brought them to where they were by that point."

Mike Gitter

"The look we had in Boston was very organic. We had the tough look down but that was partly out of necessity. We were in a cold place so we wore leather jackets, boots, jeans and hoodies. We had those sleeve hats for a while but the whole thing was utilitarian, we cut off the sleeves of our shirts to have our arms more free at shows. A lot of times we cut off not quite the whole sleeve and we'd have this extra part of material, which was perfect because the sleeve hat would cover the tops of your ears which would be freezing in the winter in Boston, but you could still show off your shaved head. You could show that you were a tough-as-nails skinhead but you could also have your ears covered."

Dave Smalley

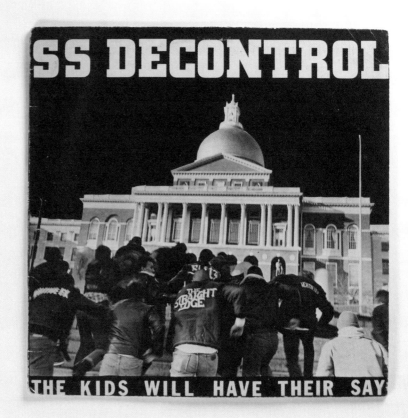

"We played our first show in Boston with Stranglehold at the height of SSD and Boston straight edge. I was standing on a chair at the back of the hall and Stranglehold went into their first song singing 'Oh the world is fucked, there is sickness and poverty etc… let's have a beer!' All of a sudden from the back came this crew with an ice chest full of beer that got passed around and was being drank and sprayed. A huge party with a great soundtrack. I remember thinking 'This is straight edge Boston?'"
<u>Tim Kerr</u>

"My first exposure to punk rock was in 1976, buying records at Discount Records in Boston's porn district known as 'The Combat Zone.' It was the only store that brought in punk. It was a trek from the suburbs but it was also a way to get your porn fill. Harvard Square was the opposite in appearance; more cultured because of the college book stores but both reeked freedom of speech and going against the norm. I'll never forget the day *The Kids Will Have Their Say* hit the stores. We had the beginnings of an army, it was our stamp, it was Boston. We now had a division and when *This is Boston Not L.A.* came out we had a full arsenal of soldiers."
<u>Curtis Casella</u>

058.063
SSD at CBGB, New York,
New York, c.1983; Photograph by
<u>Philin Phlash</u>, originally published
in *Forced Exposure* #6

"In one issue of *Forced Exposure* fanzine there was a live show review of SSD playing in Boston in 1983. In the review there was a picture of SSD, and Al Barile was wearing this black T-shirt that just said NINJA really big on it. A line from the review said '…and the karma was really flowing tonight as SSD brought down the hammer…' For me, something just clicked and I thought 'That is what a live show needs to be.' When you go on stage, it should be like a duel and not in a tough guy way at all, but like a duel against yourself and the pressures you face and your personal demons that you have to fight."

Chris Bratton

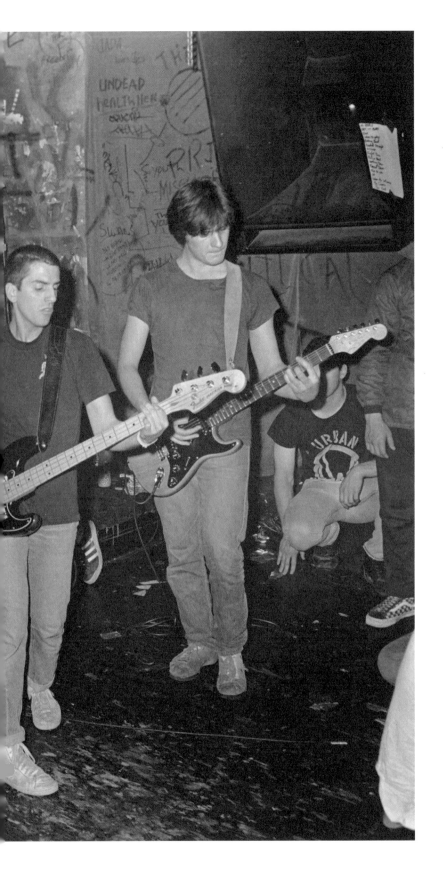

DROP DEAD
No relief
No release
No peace

None alive
None survive
genocide
drop dead (3X)
No refrain
only pain
only pain....

CONFORM
monkey see monkey do monkey has low I.Q
copy cat conform conform for the sake of your comfort
don't dare ask questions just accept blend in
conform conform do what's the norm
Proper dress required or you won't be hired.........
Bunch of fucking mindless goons listen to the same old tunes
look at me and think I'm strange
haven't got the balls to change
haven't got a mind of your own, just another zombie clone
No individuality slave of the majority
dress the same be accepted true self might be rejected
afraid to try something new, afraid of what others think
OF YOU!

LIFE of HATE
BIGOT WHITE Proud Straight
All you ever do is hate
Anyone different from you
Black gay Hispanic Jew
teach your children filthy lies
intimidate with your size
use violence to get your way
support the K.K.K.
Have no respect for others
waging war against your brothers
can't you fucking see
they're just like you and me
TAKE your white supremacy
AND GO FUCK OFF

STARVATION
No food here to find walking skeletons stand in
line for insects in a bowl of wheat stillborn
babies never eat STARVATION (4X)

Skin stretched over bone starving children
can't stand alone Flies attracted to the killed
swollen stomachs never filled STARVATION (4X)

leaders of this place running in the arms race
Buy the bombs and starve the nation
thousands dying of starvation STARVATION (4X)

GRIM REAPER
Doctor laid a doodie on my head today
Cancer eating my lung tissue away
late at night I lock the door to my room
I fear the grim reaper come to call on me soon
Nowhere to run, Nowhere to hide
bony fingers clutch my spine
Skull face swinging a sythe
Jesus Christ I want to live.....

Arms race disgrace ARMAGEDDON (2X)
peaceful claim yet bombs are aimed ARMAGEDDON (2X)
Arms are poised earth destroyed ARMAGEDDON (2X)
Nation of pain nation slain Armageddon (2X)

SIEGE

guitar ~ Bruno Habel
bass ~ Henry McNamee
drums ~ Robert Williams
voice ~ Screaming Kev Mahoney

060.064 [previous spread]
DYS at The Channel, Boston,
Massachusetts, 1983; Photograph
by Gail Rush
*DYS played this show with **SSD**.
The same night **The Misfits** filmed
their video for 'Braineaters.'*
—Gail Rush

062.065 [right]
Siege *Demo* lyric sheet, 1984;
Courtesy of Al Quint

062.066 [below]
Siege *Demo* cassette; 1984;
Courtesy of Al Quint

063.067 [opposite above]
Choke, **Slapshot** at The Chanel,
Cambridge, Massachusetts, 1987;
Photograph by JJ Gonson

063.068 [opposite below]
Wrecking Crew Cambridge,
Massachusetts, 1987; Photograph
by JJ Gonson

"In the spring of '84 Siege played a show at their high school in
Weymouth, Massachusetts. I drove nearly an hour to get there and
the asshole assistant principal wouldn't let any 'outsiders' into the
show. I don't think he was too thrilled Siege were playing to begin
with. I didn't want to risk getting arrested for trespassing and didn't
have the courage to try to weasel my way in there. I heard how Kurt
unveiled a T-shirt that said Fuck Off and how he jumped off the
stage and fucked up his ankle. Damn I wish I'd seen that."

Al Quint

"There is one band that towers over any band from the Boston area:
Siege. Four pissed kids from the South Shore that have left a musical
legacy like a boot kicking us all in the face and most people didn't
know it at the time. A metallic terror grind with the sickest vocals
you ever want to hear at the center of a sonic hurricane. Most of
the classic grindcore bands totally acknowledge them as a huge
influence. Seems that the Siege demo was copied so much that by
the time it got to the UK and into the hands Napalm Death's Mitch
Harris and Lee Dorrian the shit had sped up to a point where it was
an ugly blur of sound. Hence, serious grind was born."

Mike Gitter

"The constant influx of new collegiate types is where some of the classic Boston characters came from; Dave Smalley going to Boston College after living in Virginia, Choke moving from Provincetown, Massachusetts to go to Emerson. Every scene has its own factors that make it different; the Senator's sons in D.C., the surfer jocks of Orange County, California throwing down to Black Flag, the impoverished squatters of New York City. What made Boston was that influx of the new versus the old: The *Good Will Hunting*-townie types quietly merging with the collegiate types and creating a real identity that could only happen in that old and cold Yankee town. It was a culture clash that gave Boston its identity. What did Al Barile get called, a 'hockey jock?' Now that is Boston, not anywhere else."

Mike Gitter

064.069 [opposite]
Verbal Assault *Eyes* T-shirt, c.1987;
Design by <u>Christopher Jones</u>

065.070 [above]
Verbal Assault at T.T. the Bear's,
Cambridge, Massachusetts,
February 14, 1987; Photograph
by <u>JJ Gonson</u>

"We were really young when we did the band, in our late teens and early twenties. It was a huge advantage because we didn't have to live off the band. We still had our stuff at our folk's houses when we were on tour. We always broke even or made a little money but the finances weren't such a concern for us. The merchandise was always crucial, because it would help with the gas money and stuff like that. What really kept us right sized was living in Newport, Rhode Isand. It's a small town and close-knit community. It was hard to get your head up your ass because you were home after tour and you'd got back to being a fry cook in a restaurant to save money for school.

The eyes logo is actually Sinead O'Connor's left eye. It was a photo from the cover of *Rolling Stone*. I kept Xeroxing and Xeroxing the image until I had gotten rid of all the grey scale, and then I Xeroxed it on to a clear plastic sheet and flipped it over to create a pair of eyes. I did the type with Letraset and designed it in my dorm room when I was going to the University of Massachusetts. It came out well and it was simple color wise. It only used three colors which was important because you could print it on a dark shirt and only use two colors of ink to screen it which kept the cost of printing the shirts down. It was a lot different than having a whole catalog of fonts at your fingertips like you do with personal computers now. When you're trying to finish a flyer and you run out of lower case 'a's you would have to go to the art store to buy Letraset and hope they had Impact or whatever font you needed."

<u>Christopher Jones</u>

"I remember a 7 Seconds show, where right before it started I gave Kevin Seconds a T-shirt of my band Just Because and asked him to wear it on stage. He just said 'Yeah, no problem man' and throws it over to their roadie, this big burly guy that looked like Rollins that was at every show, he had a beard and shit. He rips the neck and arms off and throws it back to Kevin and goes 'Here you go man.' That's how Kevin Seconds wore all his shirts. Later he wore the shirt on stage and we were so stoked."

Casey Jones

DEAR IAN,

ONCE AGAIN, THANKS FOR ULTRA-COOL RECORD. 'FLEX' IS FUCKIN' KILLER! AT TIMES, A LOT, I FEEL LIKE JUST GETTIN' UP AND MOVIN' OUT THERE, BUT I KINDA HAVE A COMMITMENT TO THE SKEENO SCENE TO UPHOLD, AND SO I GOTTA STICK IT OUT, FOR AWHILE AT LEAST. NOT THAT IT'S TOTALLY FUCKED HERE OR ANYTHING, IT'S JUST SO DEAD HERE LATELY, PLUS THE FUCKING FACTIONS BACKSTABBING ONE ANOTHER. HOW FUCKING STUPID!!! I MEAN, WE GET SHIT FROM THE LOCAL IDIOTS JUST 'COS WE'RE PUTTIN' OUT A RECORD AND 'COS WE'RE POPULAR IN S.F. ETC., PLUS, TO A LOT OF THE GIRLS HERE, IF YOU SHAVE YOUR HEAD, YOU'RE A POSEUR. CAN YOU BELIEVE THAT? ANYWAY, ENOUGH OF MY BITCHIN'. IT'S JUST BEEN SO BORING AROUND HERE LATELY. NO GIGS (EXCEPT FOR THE ONES IN TAHOE — HOME OF THE GREAT URBAN ASSAULT AND NOBODY DOIN' OR SAYIN' ANYTHING NEW. OH WELL, HERE'S A TAPE WITH A BUNCHA STUFF ON IT INCLUDING MORAL DISRUPT (DON'T WANNA GET MOONSTOMPED Y'KNOW) AND OTHERS. WISH I COULD SEND YOU RECORDS (DISCHORD IS LIKE GOD HERE!! BUT SO FAR NOTHIN'S OUT YET. BUT, WHEN RELEASED I'LL SEND YOU THE RECORDS COMING OUT WITH SKEENO BANDS LIKE: 7 SECONDS 'SKINS, BRAINS, GUTS E.P.' MAXIMUM ROCK 'N' ROLL ALBUM — 7SECS, WRECKS, SEC. 8 & UR. ASSAULT (I PRODUCED!); L.A. COMPILATION ALBUM ON I.C.I. WITH SECTION 8 PLUS D.O.A., LEWD ETC. ETC. AND THE EASTERN FRONT L.P. WHICH WE MAY OR MAY NOT BE ON NOW (FUCKING SOUND ENGINEER DIDN'T RECORD US, THE FIX, SIC PLEASURE (NO BIGGIE) OR A.L.A.) ALSO, MISC. STUFF LIKE FLYERS, ETC. KEEP IN TOUCH AND TAKE CARE.

WE MIGHT BE PUTTING SOMETHING OUT ON ALTERNATIVE TENTACLES, BUT IN OUR HEART AND HEAD, IT'S DISCHORD!!!

⊕ AND X X X RULE,

KEVIN

P.S. — PLAYED WITH BAD BRAINS IN S.F. (SEE FLYER). FUCKING KILLER!!!

P.S.S. — COULD YOU INTERVIEW SAB AND IRON CROSS FOR THE NEXT SKINHEAD, OR IF YOU DON'T WANT TO ASK SOMEBODY WHO MIGHT? FANX. AND IF THERE'S ANY PHOTOS.....

STEVE AND JANE SAY HI AND MANY THANKS

066.070 [previous spread]
Black Flag at The Milestone, Charlotte, North Carolina, December 1981; Photograph by Rusty Moore

068.071 [opposite above]
Home made **7 Seconds** T-shirt, c.1986; Illustration by Jon Field

068.072 [opposite below]
Leading Edge fanzine #4 [back cover detail], 1985; Edited by Martin Sprouse, photograph by Al Flipside

069.073 [above]
Letter from Kevin Seconds to Ian MacKaye; May 4, 1982

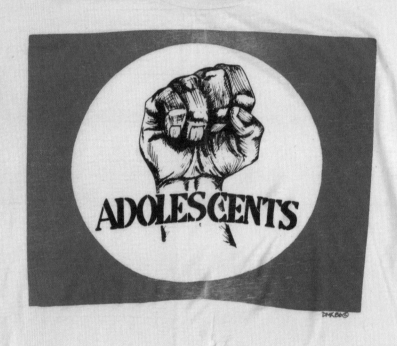

070.075 [opposite]
The Adolescents *Fist*
T-shirt, c.1986

071.076 [top]
The Adolescents at Lupo's
Heartbreak Hotel, Providence,
Rhode Island, July 27, 1986;
Photograph by JJ Gonson

071.077 [above]
Rikk Agnew, **The Adolescents**
backstage at Lupo's Heartbreak
Hotel, Providence, Rhode Island,
July 27, 1986; Photograph by
JJ Gonson

071.078 [left]
The Adolescents at Lupo's
Heartbreak Hotel, Providence,
Rhode Island, July 27, 1986;
Photograph by JJ Gonson

Skater/Musician — Brian Brannon

INDEPENDENT

072.079 [opposite]
Violent Children original artwork
for the *s/t* 7" United Nutmeg
Records 1984; Illustration by FAT

073.080 [left]
Independent Truck Company®
advertisement featuring
Brian Brannon, *Thrasher*
magazine, April 1987;
Photograph by Bryce Kanights

073.081 [below]
Ian MacKaye [skateboarding],
Brian Baker [standing], and
Unknown [kneeling], c.1983;
Photograph by Al Flipside

"I issued a skate rock challenge to a bunch of bands at a time when everyone was coming
out with skateboards with their names on them. I was like, 'Hey, wait a second. Do these
dudes even skate?' Some of it was tongue-in-cheek, like when I called out Minor Threat:
'They don't drink, they don't smoke, they don't fuck, but do they fucking skate?' I just
couldn't resist throwing that in there."

Brian Brannon

"Brian Brannon took issue to Minor Threat being called a 'skate band' and he challenged
me to a skate competition. That happened to me a lot over the years, people would say
'I bet you really suck' and I'd respond 'I never said I was good.'"

Ian MacKaye

"When JFA's first record came out I was in grammar school. When they finally came to
play New York City they came to the Pyramids in Queens, which were at the entrance
to the Con Edison plant. It was like the second coming, we thought 'Holy cow, JFA are
skating our pyramids!' We all [Token Entry] grew up a few blocks from the Pyramids.
We'd show up and blast radios and skateboard. It was so industrial and because we were
so far from the Ditmars area that no one would show up and ever tell us to leave. When
a band would come through they might have heard about it and would just show up."

Ernie Parada

074.082 [left]
Circle Jerks at Friday's, Greensboro, North Carolina; November 29, 1983; Photograph by <u>Rusty Moore</u>

074.083 [below]
Circle Jerks at Friday's, Greensboro, North Carolina. November 29, 1983; Photograph by <u>Rusty Moore</u>

075.084 [opposite]
Big Boys *Pray for me, I Don't Fit In* T-shirt, c.1982

"Playing with the Big Boys was like nothing else in the world. When they sang about 'Fun, Fun, Fun' they really meant it. No attitudes. No bullshit. Just pure old Texas hospitality with a heaping helping of twisted punk rock mentality mixed in. One of our favorite sessions was skating the Pflugerville ditch. We had read about it for years in *Thrasher*. When we finally got to ride it with Big Boys, it was a dream come true."

Brian Brannon

"The anarchy skate symbol was easier and faster to graffiti than 'Big Boys.' At some point we changed Cockney Rejects to Minor Threat. We [Big Boys] had started in '78, at the tail end of punk. That was when punk meant anything from rockabilly to crazy art synth to new wave, when the old guard tried to make an issue out of this new hardcore thing. That's where those lyrics ['Fun, Fun, Fun'] came from, a sort of middle finger with a big smartass smile to the self-appointed scene police here in town."

<u>Tim Kerr</u>

big boys
I'm a punk and I like SHAM, COCKNEY REJECTS are the worlds greatest band
but I like JOY DIVISION, PUBLIC Image too . . . even though
thats not what I'm suppose to do.

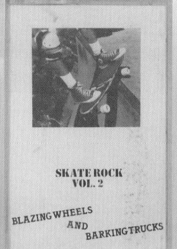

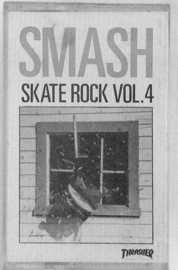

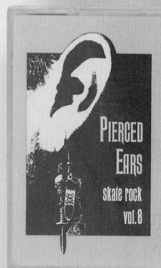

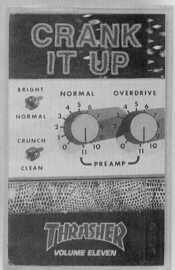

"When *Thrasher* came out it looked more like a big fanzine. It was great! When the Big Boys first went to the West Coast we got in touch with Kevin Thatcher and Mofo [*Thrasher* editor and photographer], not to be in the magazine, but to get them to take us to any ditches they knew of to skate. The similarities between the already established network of skaters and the hardcore bands was almost one-and-the-same—just folks helping other folks. It became more apparent that a lot of the bands had a skater or two in them."

Tim Kerr

"In 1981 when we started playing, everything had pretty much gone to shit. All the skateparks were closed, *Skateboarder* magazine had disintegrated, and true skateboarders were few and far between. The hard times had weeded out everyone but the hardcore skate rats who lived and breathed skateboarding. *Thrasher* magazine was born during that period and showed all of us miscreants from across the nation that we weren't alone in our struggle to skate. The term 'Skate Rock' was invented by Mofo, the O.G. photo editor for *Thrasher*, and the singer for the Drunk Injuns. It came to encompass all of the hardcore skate bands that sprouted up across the nation, as more and more bands began providing a soundtrack to shred. Every single band on those early comps was a force to be reckoned with and helped pave the way for what Skate Rock has become today."

Brian Brannon

"When I was 16, me and the other two hardcore kids in my school skated every single waking hour of every day. We didn't let the fact that we completely sucked get in our way. At the time, [skate-boarding] was considered to be a pretty weird thing by 'regular' upper middle class East Coast society. Preppy kids used to laugh at us and say 'Aren't you turds a little old to be skateboarding?' Skateboards were considered a childish novelty back then, like hula hoops. Just knowing none of the regulars at school could wrap their heads around it made me want to skate even more."

John Porcelly

"Whenever JFA would roll into a new town, we'd have a whole quiver of boards ready to go. We had downhill boards for steep hill bombs and mountain passes, street boards with soft wheels for nasty rough asphalt and shotcrete ditches, and of course our pool, pipe, and vert boards for when we got really lucky. Hanging out at the club, doing sound checks and acting like rock stars wasn't in the cards for us. We would seek out whatever local rippers we could find and ask for a ride to their spots. Usually we would get back just in time to plug in our equipment and play, or maybe even catch one of the opening acts."

Brian Brannon

Fri	1988 Mar 18	Judge, Side By Side, Project X, Up Front, Pressure Release (no Y.O.T.)
Mon	May 30 Brink+Wood	Youth of Today, Beyond
Sat	June 4	Youth of Today (video shoot), Gorilla Biscuits, Judge, Beyond
Sun	June 19	Up Front, Pressure Release, Outburst
Fri	June 24	Breakdown, Y.D.L., Powersurge (no Agnostic Front)
Fri	Aug 26	Verbal Assault, Uppercut, Wide Awake
Sat	Sept. 10	Up Front, No Outlet, Pressure Release, Our Gang
Fri	Sept 23	Gorilla Biscuits, Beyond, Wrecking Crew, Raw Deal
Fri	Oct 28	Insted, Bold, Supertouch, Wide Awake
Fri	Nov 18	Gorilla Biscuits, No For An Answer, Chain of Strength, Outburst
Fri	Dec 9 UCONN	Gorilla Biscuits, Sick of it All, Raw Deal, Laughing Hyenas, Screeching Weasel, Spongetunnel
Sat	Dec 17	Cro-Mags, Leeway, Absolution
Fri	Dec 30	Murphy's Law, Ice-Men, American Standard
Sat	1989 Mar 25	Wrecking Crew, Maximum Penalty, Powersurge (no Breakdown + Y.D.L.)
Sat	Apr 8	Token Entry, Breakdown, Seizure
Sat	May 12	Raw Deal, Warbucks, Inside-Out
Fri	June 2	Gorilla Biscuits, Sick of it All, Vision, Bad Trip
Sat	June 3	Bold, Scream, Supertouch
Fri	June 24	Token Entry, In Your Face, AWOL
Sun	July 9	Underdog, Supertouch, Sick of it All, Inside-Out, Wide Awake, Up Front, Unit Pride, Within
Sat	Oct 21	Murphy's Law, Hard-ons, Eye For an Eye, Blue Balls
Sat	Oct 28	Token Entry, AWOL
Sat	Nov 18	Killing Time, Powersurge, Crossface, Warbucks
Sat	Dec 9	Judge, Outburst, React, Intensity
Sat	1990 Jan 13 The RAT	Uppercut, Said & Done
Fri	Feb 2 UCONN	Token Entry, Supertouch, Heads Up
Fri	Feb 9	Judge, Intensity, Release, Courage
Sat	Feb 18	Killing Time, Maximum Penalty, At All Cost
Fri	Apr 20	Murphy's Law, Lunachicks, Lost Generation
Sat	May 12	Sick of it All, Supertouch, Burn, Stand Up, AWOL (no Judge)
Sat	June 9	Gorilla Biscuits, Zero Tolerance, Say no more
Sat	July 9	Judge, Insight, Payback, Billings Gate
Mon	Aug 10 RITZ	Sick of it All, Killing Time, Token Entry, Gorilla Biscuits, Supertouch, Burn, Vision, Quicksand
Fri	Aug 17 MIDDLESEX COMMUNITY COLLEGE ANTHRAX	No Doubt } Same night Verbal Assault
Fri	Aug 24	Killing Time, Sheer Terror, Payback
Sun	Sept 30 CHANNEL	Slapshot, The Mighty Mighty Bosstones, Maelstrom
Sun	Oct 7 Bunratty's	Killing Time, Sheer Terror, Said & Done
Sun	Nov 4 Bunratty's	Wrecking Crew, Quicksand, Eye For an Eye, Bloodbath
Sun	Nov 18	Shelter, Discipline, Burn, 3rd Degree, Hard as Nails
Sat	1991 Jan 12 Channel	Agnostic Front, Sick of it All, Wrecking Crew, Burn
Fri	Feb 15 Paradise	Mighty Mighty Bosstones, NY Citizens
Fri	March 1 Emerson	Eye For an Eye
Sun	March 17 Channel	Fugazi, Eye For an Eye
Sat	March 23 UCONN	Murphy's Law
Sun	Apr. 7 Bunratty's	Sick of it All, Vision, Crawlpappy, Kingpin
Sun	Apr 28	Eye For an Eye, Born Against, Rorshach, 3rd Degree (Insted)
Sun	May 12 Paradise	Cro-Mags (John Bloodclot), Wrecking Crew, Sam Black Church, Burn

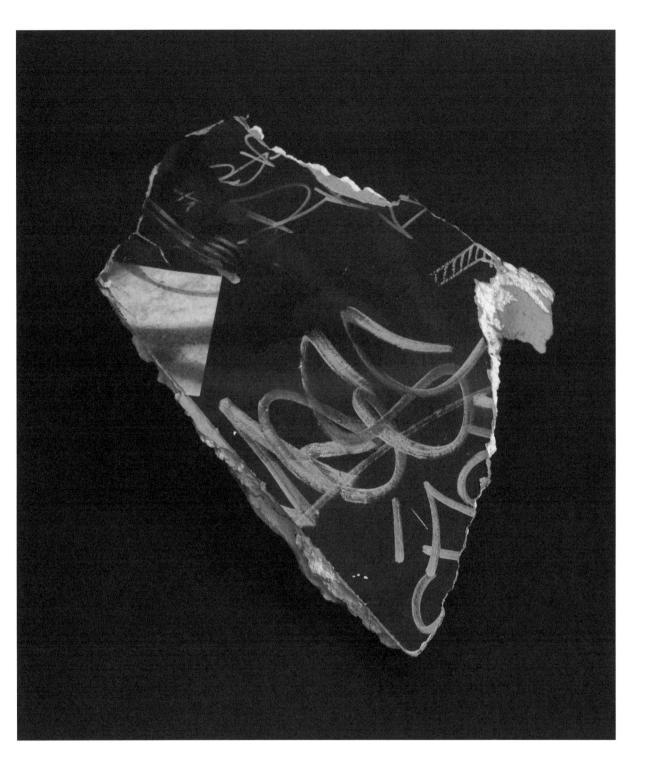

"Two things made the Anthrax different than almost any other club I've ever been to—the fact that it was always all ages (no alcohol), and that the owners, Brian and Shaun, and the staff were fans of the music, just like me. The worst thing was when your parents came early to pick you up and the sound guy Bill [from 76% Uncertain] had to call your name over the PA system. He would be like 'Yo, Mike Torrelli… Is that the right name Shaun? Mike Torrelli, if you're here, come back here and talk to me… I have a message for you. I don't want to embarrass you and tell you that your parents are waiting for you outside, so come back and I'll tell you.'"

<u>Jon Field</u>

"The last show at the Anthrax [Friday November 2, 1990] the walls were being pulled down piece by piece. The following day some friends and I drove back for one last look, and I found a piece of the wall in a dumpster outside. If the heart of the Anthrax was the stage then the soul was outside among the station wagons, flyers, and empty cans of Jolt."

<u>Luke Hoverman</u>

"The early New York style was leather jackets, Dr. Martens, shaved heads. Very much the skinhead image you'd associate with Agnostic Front. What changed that look was Youth of Today bringing the suburban thing with them. We were kids from New York but we were dressing like kids from Connecticut. We wore Champion sweatshirts and varsity jackets. Youth of Today really connected with suburban kids, whereas I don't think the Cro-Mags did in that same way. Youth of Today's logo was a fist, it projected strength in a way that you wouldn't want to fuck with the high school football, not the same as some dudes on a street corner in the Lower East Side, they're probably more down to knife you."

Walter Schreifels

"The 'youth crew' look became an obsession to get this conformist attire. Everyone had their hooded sweatshirts, rolled-up jeans and 19 pairs of sneakers. When things spread out to the suburbs a lot of the bands were suburban kids who were living at home. They had money to spend on this stuff. It's really easy to rally behind that when you're young but it's also a lot like a gang mentality. It's nice to have somewhere to fit in, but just as quickly there were people like myself that stepped out of high school into these dark clubs that were scary and cool, and I found myself in the same high school clique all over again. I quickly tried to move out of that because it didn't excite me anymore. When that happened I lost a lot of friends. People started asking 'What are you doing? You're not putting Xs on your hands anymore, you're going out with this girl and having a good time, you're wearing boots again?!'"

Drew Thomas

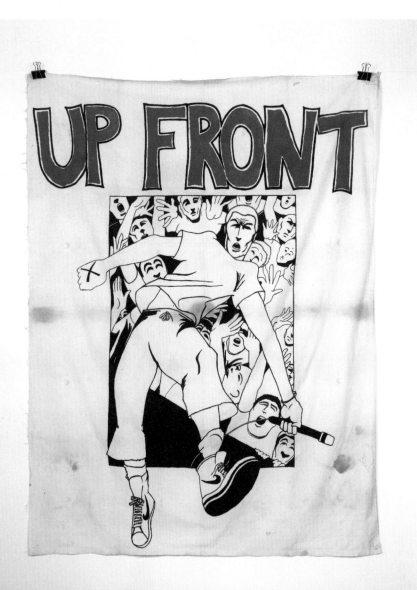

082.091 [above]
X-Rated, Swatch®, 1987; Swatch® only produced the X-Rated for one year.
Youth of Today's John Porcelly is often credited as the first person to popularize the X-Rated Swatch® in the straight edge scene.

082.092 [left]
Up Front banner, 1988; Original illustration by Russ Braun, redrawn by Jon Field
*Back in the late 1980s everyone had two things, a banner and an intro. When our friend Russ came up with a great new T-shirt design, I immediately started making a banner out of it. I set up shop in my parent's living room for a few days with the new T-shirt design, an old white sheet, a fat Magnum permanent marker and a ruler. The banner was so big it wouldn't even fit on my bedroom floor. —*Jon Field

SCHISM POLL 1987 !

BEST BAND OF 1987 _____

WORST BAND OF 1987 _____

MOST IMPROVED BAND OF 1987 _____

BEST 'ZINE OF 1987 _____

WORST 'ZINE OF 1987 _____

BEST ALBUM OF 1987 _____

WORST ALBUM OF 1987 _____

BEST SINGLE OF 1987 _____

WORST SINGLE OF 1987 _____

BEST RECORD STORE OF 1987 _____

WORST RECORD STORE OF 1987 _____

BEST CLUB OF 1987 _____

WORST CLUB OF 1987 _____

BIGGEST ASSHOLE OF 1987 _____

BEST SHOW OF 1987 _____

ARE YOU STRAIGHT EDGE ? _____

ARE YOU A SKINHEAD ? _____

ARE YOU A VEGETARIAN ? _____

DO YOU HAVE ANY TATOOS ? _____

DO YOU COLLECT RECORDS ? _____

WHAT KIND OF FOOTWEAR DO YOU WEAR ? _____

BEST VOCALIST OF ALL TIME _____

BEST GUITARIST OF ALL TIME _____

BEST BASSIST OF ALL TIME _____

BEST DRUMMER OF ALL TIME _____

FAVORITE DISCHORD RECORD _____

LEAST FAVORITE DISCHORD RECORD _____

083.093 [left]
Schism poll, 1987

083.094 [below]
John Porcelly at the Schism
house, Brooklyn, New York, 1988;
Photograph by ROA

"The Schism house was Al Brown's and my apartment in Brooklyn, New York. It was like a non-stop straight edge party. The front room had a rotating *Seinfeld*-like cast of characters. Pretty much our only occupation was folding Judge *New York Crew* sleeves.

Williamsburg was a lot different then. It definitely was not the hipster neighborhood it is today. I'd ride my bike back to Brooklyn over the Williamsburg bridge to get home. There were drug dealers selling crack right on the bridge, so you'd have to dodge junkies trying to steal the bike out from underneath you on they way home. Bands used to come through all the time and crash at our place."

John Porcelly

"Porcell asked me to move into the Schism house when I was 18-years-old, just two months out of high school. I had a girlfriend in Brooklyn so I wanted to be there and was already traveling from Long Island all the time. I lived with those guys and saw what they were doing with Schism. I'd jam with Porcell, he'd be writing Judge songs in his part of the house, I'd be writing stuff for Bold in my part, and Alex would be painting and doing art all the time."

Tom Capone

084.095 [above]
Outside **Killing Time's** "last" show,
CBGB New York, New York 1990.
Photograph by <u>Glenn Maryansky</u>
*Not the last show Killing Time
played, but their "first" last show.*
—GLENN MARYANSKY

085.096 [opposite]
**Straight Ahead, Absolution, Side
by Side,** and **Raw Deal** at CBGB.
January 2, 1989; Photographs by
<u>Theresa Kelliher</u>

"We [Beyond] felt like a minor league team, but if you played CBGB you were the Yankees. When we were invited to play there it felt like winning a Grammy. My parents came in a Lincoln Continental. They pulled up to the Bowery right next to the rasta flop house and we were just psyched because nothing happened to their car."

Vic DiCara

"In the early '80s my brother would bring home Judas Priest, Iron Maiden, Motörhead, stuff like that. I liked the aggression but once I heard punk and hardcore I liked the idea that they were speaking about reality-based stuff. To me, I could feel it a lot more. The music was simpler, it wasn't this puff of smoke. I got into the Bad Brains and Minor Threat in '82 and went to my first show in '84. By the summer of '84 I was playing CBGB. Boom, right away, it was right there. New York has a very 'street' attitude. When you're crammed up in everyone's face, it's all back and forth and I think that really translates in the music.

Shortly after we put the Straight Ahead 12" out Tommy and I had a disagreement and we broke up and I joined Agnostic Front. We were very on and off which is probably why we weren't documented that much. We did things in these short bursts and that's what kept it exciting because it was like unfinished business. It made an impression on the kids that were around then because we had a real urgency. When we performed live it was so energetic, it was just teetering on the edge but that's what made it exciting too."

Craig Setari

STRAIGHT AHEAD · ABSOLUTION ·
SIDE BY SIDE · RAW DEAL

DATE 2 Jan '89   ASSIGNMENT   FILE NO. CBGB'S

SHOOT FROM THIS TYPE

NEW YORK CITY HARDCORE   39%
T H E   W A Y   I T   I S

T H E   W A Y   I T   I S

REVELATION RECORDS PRESENTS
NEW YORK CITY
HARDCORE

086.097 [opposite above]
Gorilla Biscuits at the Anthrax,
Norwalk, Connecticut, January
15, 1988; Photograph by <u>BJ Papas</u>

086.098 [opposite below]
Original type lock-up **New York
City Hardcore:** *The Way It Is*
compilation 12", Revelation
Records, 1988; Typography
by <u>David Bett</u>

087.099 [below]
New York City Hardcore:
The Way It Is compilation 12",
Revelation Records, 1988;
Design by <u>David Bett</u>

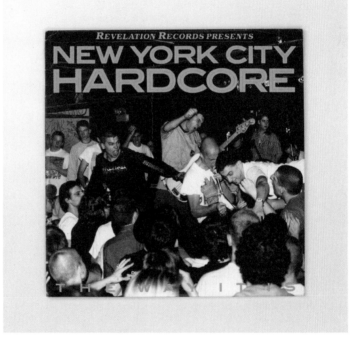

"BJ's photograph on the cover of *The Way It Is* captures the hardcore scene at that time perfectly. The show was Side by Side, Gorilla Biscuits, and Project X at the Anthrax. There might have been another band but I can't remember. It was a secret performance for Project X, as they only had a few songs to play. There were only 10 long sleeve Schism shirts there that night. You can see Al Brown wearing one, and Porcell wore one during the Project X set. I felt like I was wearing some sort of gang colors. That was the electricity I felt that night. The hardcore scene had gotten bigger and it just felt like a huge party with all of our friends."

<u>Gus Peña</u>

"Youth of Today, they were probably the beginning of the trend of there not being just four guys on stage. Everyone they knew was on stage. After a while it became frustrating, but at that time it was like 'Look at the crew they have and look at how into it they all are!' They had this huge army of followers and their heads were all in the right spot."

<u>Ernie Parada</u>

"[The Fugazi song] 'Merchandise' was a response to the overarching emphasis on merchandise at shows in the mid-1980s. At these shows there was so much energy going into these bands selling stuff that in my mind the whole point of the music became trivialized. They were practicing this standard capitalist form of drawing in clientele. You draw in an audience and they become your clientele. It was like the old snake oil salesman. They would travel through the frontier and they'd have a caravan of musicians, acrobats or whatever. They'd set up in the middle of a town and do a show. People would gather and in between the acts the 'doctor' would come out with his various tinctures and oils which were all alcohol, essentially. This is exactly the same story in bars today. The idea that you have to see a band in a bar is so odious. It's actually that same practice, music being used as a shill to sell other products."

Ian MacKaye

088.100
Fugazi at Irving Plaza, New York,
New York; February 4, 1995;
Photograph by Glenn Maryansky

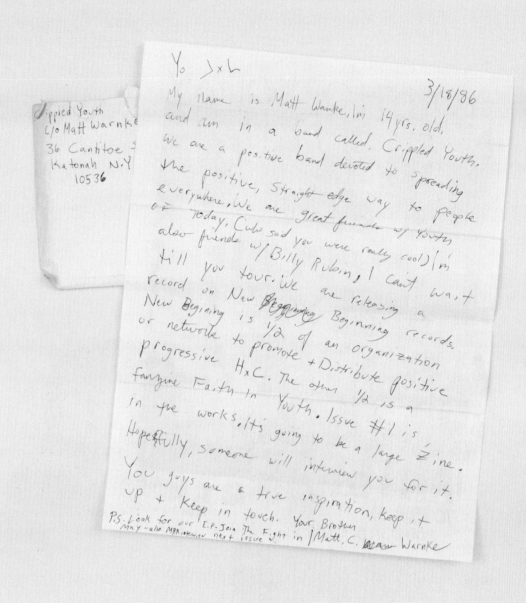

090.101 [opposite above]
090.102 [opposite below]
Crippled Youth at the Rathskeller, Boston, Massachusetts, May 11, 1986; Photograph by JJ Gonson

091.103 [above]
Letter from Matt Warnke to Casey Jones, March 18, 1986

"…Crippled Youth, Youth of Today, and Youth Brigade at the Rat in Boston. That was the 'Youth' show. We had heard about the old New York versus Boston rivalries from back in the SSD days, so we would always show up to Boston with a whole crew ready to take over the pit. I even wore my BEAT HARVARD shirt to that show. We were young, confrontational, and had a lot to prove. I remember almost beating the fuck out of Steve Risteen from Slapshot a few times, but he backed down."

John Porcelly

"Before going to my first hardcore show, I remember making stuff [T-shirts, jackets] myself to wear out. This was even before we started playing as Crippled Youth. Matt and I would go to shows and we really liked the idea of breaking out of everything that was so conformist. Looking back on it, I really liked Crippled Youth and that aesthetic. It was more punk, it was about making things and bringing them to the table without them becoming too manufactured"

Drew Thomas

092.104 [top]
Uniform Choice flyer, c.1986;
Illustrator <u>Unknown</u>

092.105 [above right]
Uniform Choice mesh hat, 1988

092.106 [above left]
Uniform Choice, Orange County,
1985; Photograph by <u>Casey</u> <u>Jones</u>

093.107 [opposite]
Wishingwell Records T-shirt
test print, c.1986

"Pat [Dubar] would do the art and I was the merchandise guy. I would print stickers, hats, sweat-pants… I was just into doing it and doing it well. We'd print every part of the shirt to give people more for their money. We could give a band this whole presentation… It was a blueprint we made up and it snowballed from there."

Courtney Dubar

"We all knew each other and had a network, but when the Dubars and Wishingwell broke, it changed all of Orange County. The national perception [of California] was based on what Wishingwell did. The Dubars showed everyone that it could be done and that it was tangible. For a scene to survive you needed that epicenter. Wishingwell Records became our identity and blueprint."

Dan O'Mahony

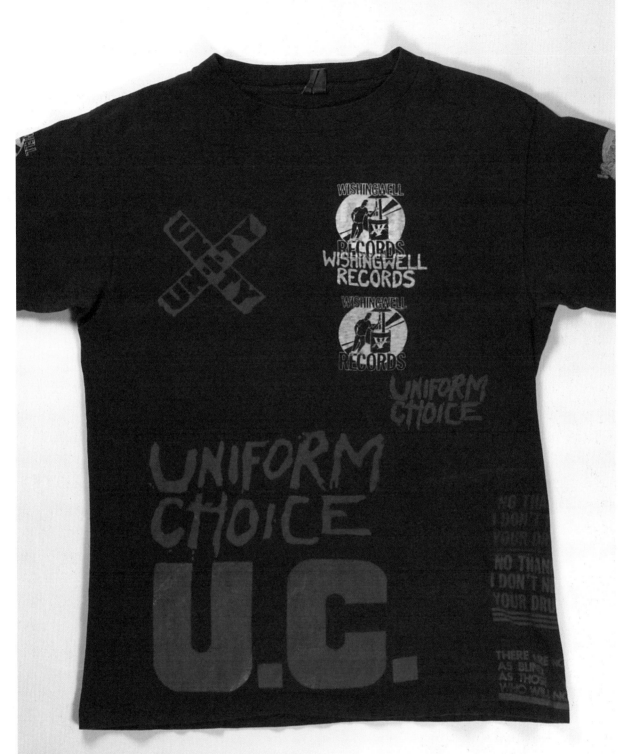

094.108 [opposite]
Pat Dubar, c.1985; Illustration
by Gavin Ogelsby, courtesy
of Pat Dubar

095.109 [above]
Uniform Choice promotional
photos, Somerville, Massachusetts.
1987; Photograph by JJ Gonson
*This was my roof in Somerville.
I was taking photographs for the
'Staring Into the Sun' record. We
spent a full day shooting photographs
all around town with my medium
format camera. I took the shoot
really seriously and borrowed
lighting equipment from my college.
It was pitch black on the roof. I'd hit
the flash and tell the guys to move,
but Pat [Dubar] wasn't into it
and didn't move, so he is the only
one who isn't double exposed.*
—JJ GONSON

"Pat Dubar would show up to a show with the hood on his sweatshirt pulled over his head and you knew underneath he was Bic bald but he wouldn't show it. Then as soon as the first song started he'd flip the hood off and people would go crazy."

Dan O'Mahony

"I took chances because I didn't have anything to prove. We grew up in a situation where there wasn't a lot of physical affection because of how my dad was raised. He didn't let himself be vulnerable. He was amazing, he worked hard for us, but it was more or less him saying 'Fucking sack up, get shit done, don't be a fucking baby, make it happen'. Being vulnerable was hard, being tough was laughable."

Pat Dubar

"Those songs for the second album sounded so different and so powerful live. I don't think they made a conscious decision to change their sound, it was just produced a certain way. They were still the same guys, they were still supporting hardcore but the delivery was totally different."

Gavin Ogelsby

REVELATION RECORDS
60 C Skiff St. Suite 886
Hamden, CT 06517

Dave, Judge came out excellently. Thanks. I don't know if you've noticed but you're doing things that you said were "too obvious" when we were first doing the NYHC comp. It's good to see. The back of the Judge LP looks almost exactly like the original pressing of Y.O.T. "Break Down the Walls" which, ~~& (that)~~ you showed me as an example of poor design because the layout was "too obvious"! I guess we like it obvious. The music & lyrics are, so why not the artwork. Enclosed is the Balance Due on Rev #15 & two good records.
Take Care, Jordan

I'm in Europe till 11/20/89

096.110 [opposite]
Note from Jordan Cooper
to David Bett, c.1989;
Courtesy of David Bett

097.111 [above]
Gorilla Biscuits at CBGB.
New York, New York, c.1989;
Photograph and hand coloring
by Theresa Kelliher

098.112 [following spread]
Gorilla Biscuits *Start Today* 12",
production mechanical;
Revelation Records, 1989;
Designed by David Bett

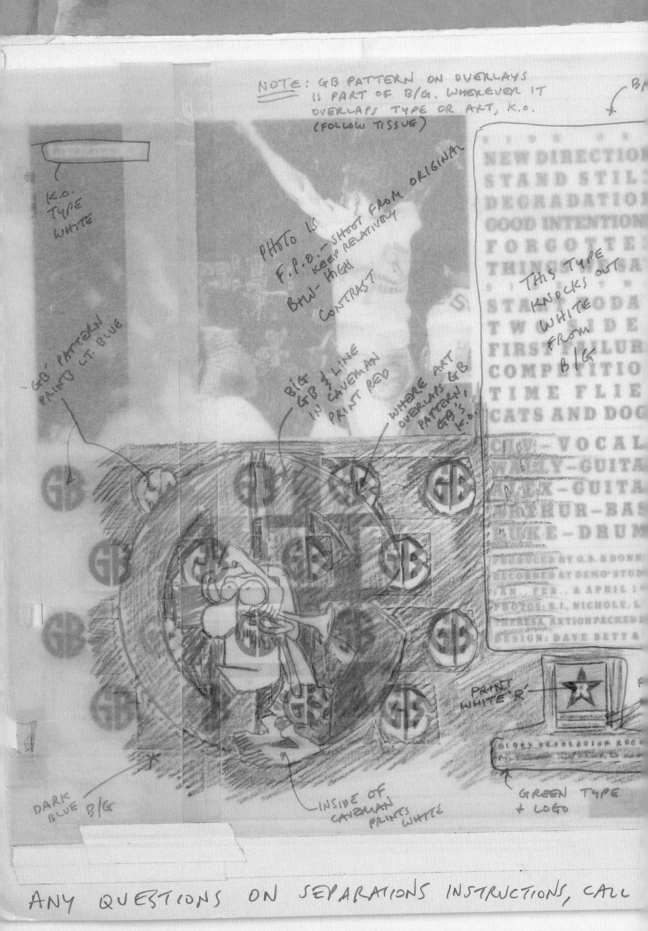

We're aiming for a different goal / Succeeding where the hippies failed / But one thing's sure and you can bet / We'll be more than a drugged-out threat!

7 Seconds "Clenched Fists, Black Eyes"

102.113 [above]
Chain of Strength at Spanky's
Cafe, Riverside, California, 1989;
Photograph by <u>Dave Sine</u>

103.114 [opposite]
Chain of Strength *True Till Death*
T-shirt, c.1988. Design by <u>Chris
Bratton</u> and <u>Ryan Hoffman</u>,
tie-dyed by <u>Malcom Tent</u> at
Trash American Style
*The original Chain of Strength shirt
was designed by Ryan and myself.
Its legendary font is a rather obvious
homage to* **SSD***, and the bracket bars
is a common straight edge hardcore
tribute to the immortal* **Run DMC***.
The shirt made it's debut August 11th,
1988 at Chain's first show in Pomona,
California.* — CHRIS BRATTON

"The original Chain of Strength songs were written lean, clean and mean for maximum stage damage. The look was focused, like no tie-dyed shirts or whatever. One of the goals of second wave in general was to be tightly focused like a laser and see just how big and worldwide this thing could get.

    The green theme went all the way back to the *Reach Out* era of Justice League. Over the years we stayed at the *Maximumrocknroll* house several times and Tim Yohannon had a world famous record collection in the lower room where he would let touring bands stay. To ensure that no one would be tempted to steal any of his valuable records, Tim had marked the borders of all his records with forest green duct tape. Justice League thought it would be funny to print a green border on the cover of *Reach Out* so it would already come with a *MRR* green duct tape cover. We were also into The Smiths *The Queen Is Dead* and *Meat Is Murder* albums which heavily featured forest green on the front and back covers. When we made the *True Till Death* 7" artwork we decided that green, white and black were our colors. To this day I hate the blue *What Holds Us Apart* cover. I think the blue looks like some other band."

<u>Chris Bratton</u>

"Zack would get so wound up that towards the end of the set, he would be singing, full-fucking-throttle screaming, with tears streaming down his face. The really intense thing is that almost always, people in the audience would be screaming the lyrics and crying too. We didn't even have a record out yet. We'd heard about this happening in D.C. when Rites of Spring played, but we didn't really believe it. When you see a room full of that kind of electricity right in front of you, it's unreal and even sort of spooky. Inside Out represented absolute, pure total fucking release, and in a really simple way. That's what the name means. We found out, years later, that Zack really does have a lot of demons and he was dancing with them right in front of us."

Chris Bratton

104.115 [opposite above]
Inside Out at Gilman Street,
Berkeley, California, summer 1989;
Photograph by <u>Dave Sine</u>

104.116 [opposite below]
No For An Answer at The Country
Club, Reseda, California, 1989;
Photograph by <u>Dave Sine</u>

105.117 [below]
Against the Wall at Spanky's
Cafe, Riverside, California, 1989;
Photograph by <u>Dave Sine</u>

"The idea Zack had was to inject an older D.C. influence back into hardcore with more complicated riffs. His idea and personality was so introspective, the name Inside Out was meant to be taken as wearing what's inside you outside so you're not hiding anything. We needed a new venue for shows and Ryan from Chain found this Persian restaurant called Spanky's. Two notes into the first song we had to stop because the owner freaked out, he thought the restaurant would be destroyed with everyone dancing and going crazy. Ryan told him that everyone would sit down, so the whole crowd sat down Indian-style and watched Inside Out play. It was so intense because with no distractions you knew everyone was watching every move you made."

<u>Vic DiCara</u>

KRISHNA BEADS

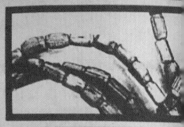

It's getting tough to go to a show lately without seeing "Krishna beads." Since they're getting so popular, my friend Gus asked me to write a short article and give a little info on them. So I'll give it a shot.

Although most popularly known in hardcore as "Krishna beads" they are more widely known throughout the world as Tulasi beads. Here's where it starts getting far out: Tulasi is a plant who is one of the purest of the purest devotees of Krishna. It might seem pretty weird that a plant would be considered a pure devotee, but devotional service and spiritual consciousness is not dependent on the type of body you have, man/woman, black/white, catholic/protestant, or even plant. Tulasi is one of the greatest devotees, and her particular relationship with Krishna is experienced in the form of a plant. From this we get a vivid example that anyone can become advanced in Krishna consciousness, even in the form of a plant it is possible.

So Tulasi, she serves Krishna and His devotees in many different ways. Her leaves are said to be very pleasing to Him and are always found decorating His feet and His food. She also provides the devotees, from her larger branches, with beads used for

meditating on the sound of Krishna's name. And, from her smaller branches, she gives everyone Krishna neck beads.

These beads are worn for many different reasons, ranging from far out to further out. But most practically, wearing Tulasi is a reminder that we have made the free choice to become serious about spiritual life and coming closer to Krishna. And that we should try to help all living entities along their path of spiritual progression.

Further, Tulasi is constantly reminding us that we are not supposed to be a bound and shackled slave to our senses, but that we are actually something which is above the senses, that we are spiritual beings who exist in an unbreakable relationship of love with the Supreme Spiritual Being who is often called Krishna, "The person who is attractive to everyone." Someone may say, "You might be into Krishna, but I'm not. So how can He be attracting everyone?" The answer is either you attracted directly to the personal form of Krishna Himself, or you are attracted to Krishna's energy, the material world and the sense gratification thereof. Either you're attracted to directly to Krishna, or indirectly to Krishna, through His energy. The more indirect the attraction, the

less pleasurable. But everyone attracted. And Tulasi tries remind us of this fact: We attracted to Krishna one way another, and the best way, most satisfying way is attraction a direct loving relationship with Him, which Tulasi wants to inspire us to explore.

Another reason for wearing Tulasi is that when people Tulasi beads, they are reminded Krishna, and for that short time they engage their mind in thinking about Him and in this simple way their spiritual consciousness benefited little by little.

So Tulasi bead simultaneously serve two purposes; they remind ourselves of our commitment spiritual life, inspiring protecting us in so many ways; they also are meant for the well of others, maybe to shake them up a little bit, or to inspire their curiosity, etc.

There is so much more to say about Tulasi. But I honestly unqualified. I've tried to explain little bit about her, but describing such a great personality is difficult to say the least. Anyway, I hope you enjoyed this article maybe understand a little more about "Krishna beads."

19

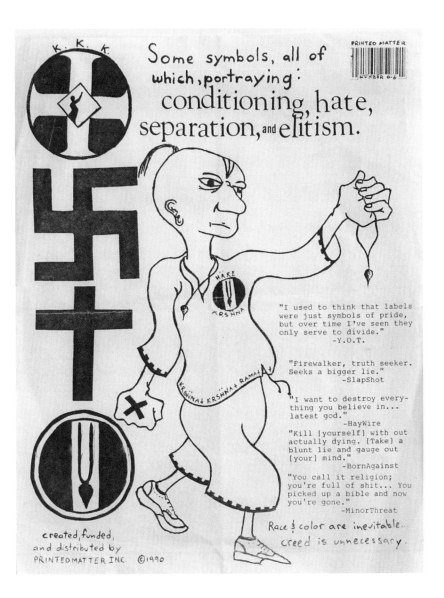

Some symbols, all of which, portraying: conditioning, hate, separation, and elitism.

K. K. K.

PRINTED MATTER
NUMBER 0-6

HARE KRSHNA

KRSHNA+ KRSHNA+ RAMA+

"I used to think that labels were just symbols of pride, but over time I've seen they only serve to divide."
-Y.O.T.

"Firewalker, truth seeker. Seeks a bigger lie."
-SlapShot

"I want to destroy everything you believe in... latest god."
-HayWire

"Kill [yourself] with out actually dying. [Take] a blunt lie and gauge out [your] mind."
-BornAgainst

"You call it religion; you're full of shit... You picked up a bible and now you're gone."
-MinorThreat

Race & color are inevitable... creed is unnecessary.

created, funded, and distributed by PRINTED MATTER INC. ©1990

106.118 [opposite]
Enquirer fanzine #4, 1990;
Published by Vic DiCara

107.119 [above]
Anti-Hare Krishna flyer for
Printed Matter fanzine, 1990;
Illustration by Robert Mars

"The first show of the tour was at the Anthrax in Connecticut, and the Born Against crew came out with flyers to incite us. They wanted to protest but their platform was flawed. They had a flyer trying to link Krishnas and their images to Nazis because the Swastika is an Indian symbol. They could have picked anything but they chose this ridiculous argument and it was a battle we could easily win."

Vic DiCara

"In 1990 I was a roadie on the Shelter, Inside Out, Quicksand tour. Shelter had a separate van for the women because, according to Krishna, they were not allowed to ride with the men. Before Shelter would play they'd have a bunch of devotees dancing and chanting in the crowd, and blowing conch shells and shit. Shelter had this guru guy who rode in their van and just sat in this big chair, and he'd spin around to face you and it. He looked like Dr. Evil in *Austin Powers*."

Joe Nelson

"The Cro-Mags had hard lives. They lived in squats in the hardest neighborhoods. When they were approached to come to the temple by the Krishnas, it addressed a need they had: food. Shelter took it to a different level they addressed the need of socialization. Shelter Krishna wasn't as scary as Cro-Mags Krishna. Ray is a little guy in stature who looked like a Hare Krishna. He wasn't this big intimidating tattooed guy. Ray and Shelter had credibility and that's what made it take off."

Gus Peña

"In 1989 when Youth of Today finished our European tour, we were at the top of our game in tightness and popularity. We had a band meeting after the last show and realized we had pretty much achieved everything we ever wanted to do with the band and much more. So we decided to go out on a high note. The *Disengage* 7" was our swan song. It was an emotional record for me because I was just a kid when the band started, so it literally felt like my youth was coming to a close as we finished that record. It was time to grow up and do something different."

John Porcelly

"Youth of Today was the first band we really all connected with in Albany [New York]. Porcell was going to school in upstate New York, and Ray was in school in Connecticut so Albany was equidistant. Ray would come up on weekends and Youth of Today would practice in our basement, which was sort of their second home. Porcell was down all the time and we'd make crazy crank phone calls. People would come back to fake messages from Harley about the brawl on the corner with the eight ball in sock. We were kids that what we did."

Dave Stein

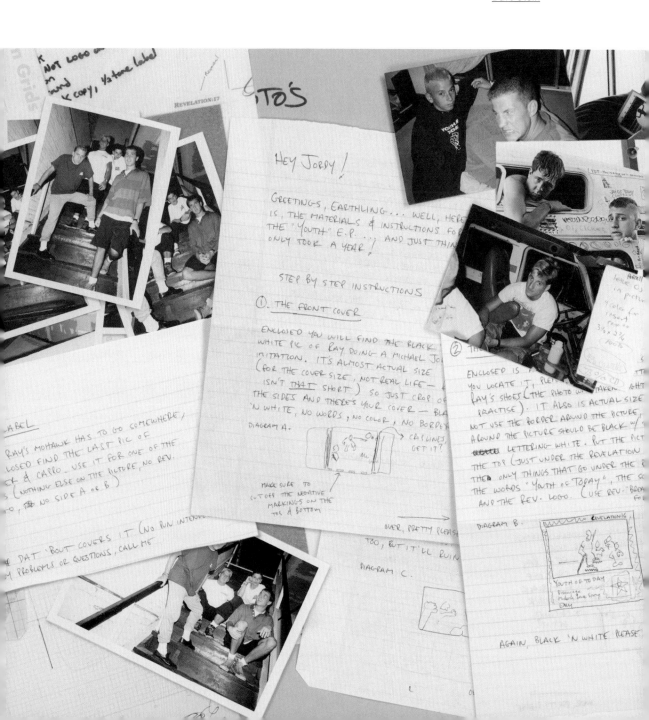

108.120 [opposite]
John Porcelly's layout instructions
for the **Youth of Today** *Disengage*
7", 1990; Courtesy of Jordan
Cooper

109.121 [left]
Youth of Today *Disengage* 7",
production mechanical; Revelation
Records, 1990; Art direction
by John Porcelly, design by
Jordan Cooper

"I think we [Agnostic Front] were naïve and short-sighted, we wouldn't take 500 dollars a night to open for a bigger band when we could make 2,500 dollars to headline the same show. Metal guys would take that loss. In the late '80s metal bands started doing package tours. You'd have Venom and Voivod touring together and sharing a backline. Instead of these bands playing one night at a smaller venue, they'd headline Madison Square Garden. Imagine if we sat down and organized a package tour of Agnostic Front, Cro-Mags, Murphy's Law, and Sick of It All in 1989. That was the difference between being a cult band and really breaking through. I always thought the Cro-Mags were so close to becoming a mega huge band and wondered what would have happened if some savvy marketers had gotten a hold of them."

Steve Martin

"Albany was a totally different scene from New York City because the kids were younger and we were more sheltered. We all lived at home, we had food, and we were all in school at some level. The New York City bands loved to play Albany because they were treated well, they got paid well, and they always got a place to stay so Albany became their second home. We tried intentionally to do things differently and make it more fun. Sometimes we'd have Twister games outside the shows, we'd do stupid stuff like that. For a long period of time we'd do matinees then everyone would head over to Chuck E. Cheese and I'd get to wear the mouse outfit. It would be like, 50 kids showing up there with Warzone or Agnostic Front. It was totally fun and different than what was going on in the city. You weren't going to go to Chuck E. Cheese after a show at CBGB."

Dave Stein

112.124 [below]
The Abused *Loud and Clear* 7";
Abused Music, 1983. Illustration
by <u>Kevin Crowley</u>

113.125 [opposite]
Leeway at CBGB, New York,
New York, 1988; Photograph
by <u>Theresa Kelliher</u>

"The Abused's *Loud and Clear* is one of the records that made me want to move to New York City. I bought it at Bleecker Bob's early on in high school, and me and the other members of my first band, The Young Republicans, used to listen to it and literally mosh around the bed and stage dive off the dresser, dreaming about hitting up A7 or CBGB one day. The walls of my room definitely started closing in on me when I listened to it. I was this sheltered suburban kid, and that 7" made the city seem exciting, artistic, dangerous and the place I wanted to be."

<u>John Porcelly</u>

"There was a mystery to a lot of the characters like Tommy Carroll then. Tom Capone would talk to him but I never did. He was a really scary guy and an imposing figure, and not just in a physical sense either, there was a mystery to him. These types of characters were a product of New York City at that time."

<u>Kevin Egan</u>

Lower East Side Crew

114.126 [above]
Warzone *Lower East Side Crew* 7",
[Lion sleeve]; Revelation Records,
1987; *A Lion Attacking a Horse*
painting by George Stubbs, c.1765,
Yale University Art Gallery, New
Haven, Connecticut, design
by <u>Jordan Cooper</u>
Six of these covers were hand made
by <u>Jordan Cooper</u> to give to the
band and friends.

114.127 [right]
Warzone *Lower East Side Crew* 7",
Revelation Records, 1987. Design
by <u>Jordan Cooper</u>

115.128 [opposite above]
Warzone at CBGB, New York,
New York, 1988; Photograph
by <u>JJ Gonson</u>

115.129 [opposite below]
Warzone *Lower East Side Crew*
T-shirt, c.1987

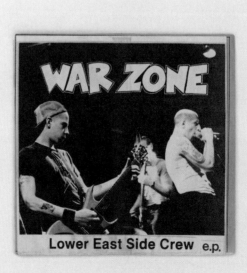

"Raybeez was such a great performer and had such a great imagination. He would do crazy show-biz type of shit in a way that really connected with the audience. I thought it was heartfelt. He really had a lot of zip and energy.

One time Raybeez showed me these [Warzone] T-shirts and asked, 'What do you think of the T-shirts bro?' I said 'Yeah, they look fucking awesome! I love it man, the iron cross, everything. It looks great, but dude, what does L.E.S. mean?' I could tell he was sad for a second and goes 'It means Lower East Side bro.' He didn't make me feel bad. He was totally cool, but he was thinking 'I got a fucking kid from Queens here!'"
Walter Schreifels

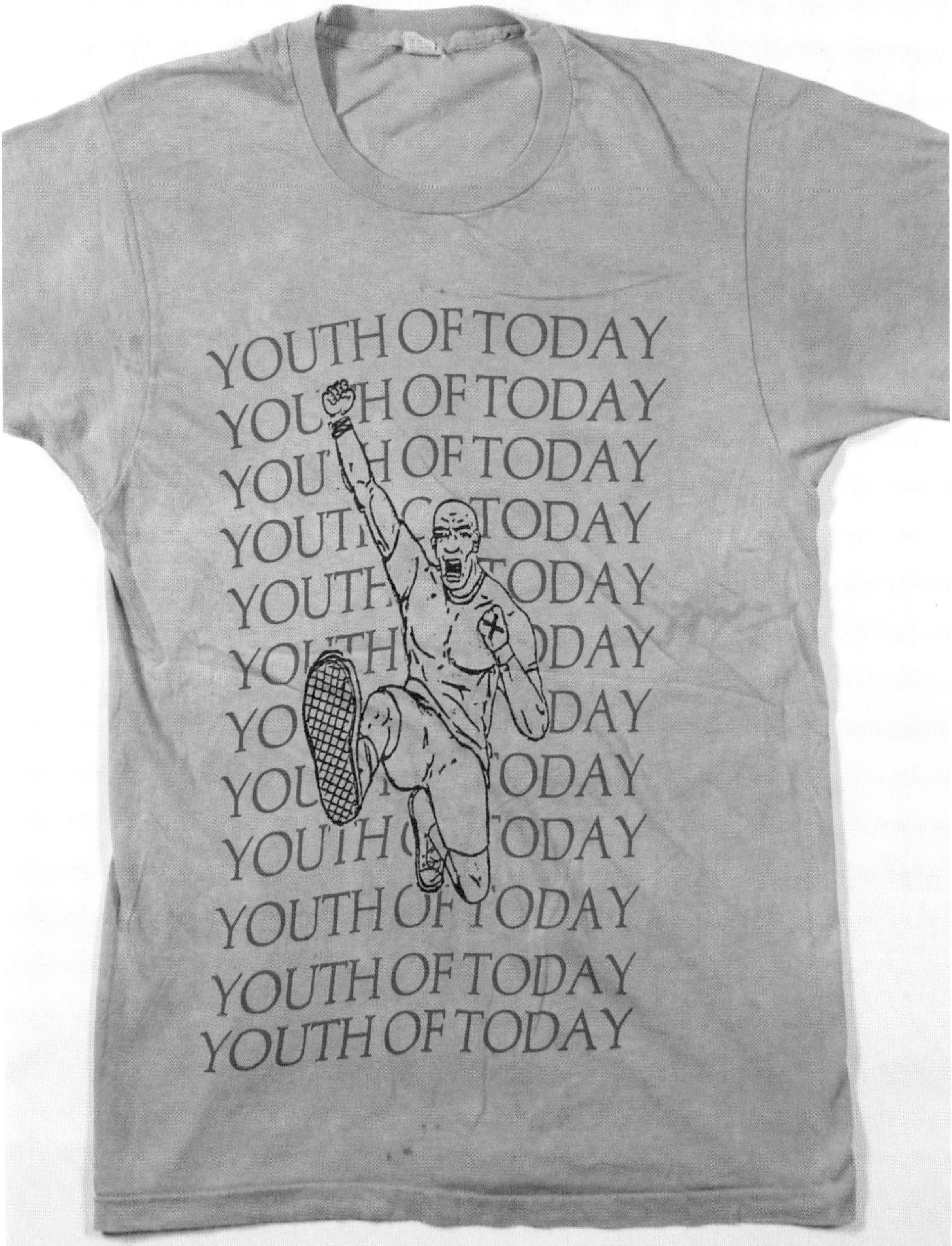
YOUTH OF TODAY
YOUTH OF TODAY
YOUTH OF TODAY
YOUTH OF TODAY

"I saw a sign on a lamppost for Some Records selling 7" punk and hardcore. It wasn't even a record store yet. They were at the flea market on Broadway. You'd go to Some before a show and Duane always had the latest demo tapes. It was an accomplishment if you had your record there because he didn't take everything. Duane closed the store because he wasn't making money. It was the coming of the compact disc, they were expensive and he was a real vinyl guy. CBGB stopped doing matinees and it really hurt him because people weren't coming by."

Dave Stein

116.130 [opposite]
Youth of Today *Some Records Shirt* exclusive T-shirt, c.1987; Illustration by <u>Dan O'Mahony</u>, design by <u>John Porcelly</u>
This shirt was printed backwards with the front graphic appearing on the back and the back graphic on the front. The shirt was dyed purple by one of the owners in the late 1980s. This exact shirt appears on the inside gatefold of the **Bold** *Speak Out* 12"

117.131 [top]
Some Records handbill, c.1986

118.132 [above]
Think fanzine #4; 1986; Edited by <u>Billy Rubin</u>, illustration by <u>Dan O'Mahony</u>

"Any scene has to have a place where people can come together, and Some Records was the club-house for New York hardcore. Duane was such a humble guy, pretty much the anti-businessman, selling records and demos for barely over the original cost. Cappo first hit him up with the idea of doing exclusive shirt designs to generate some much-needed cash flow. This [Youth of Today] shirt was sold only at Some. Dan O'Mahony did the drawing. I remember taking that fanzine to Kinko's, copying the picture, cutting out the flag with scissors and redrawing the hand, and putting it all together in about three minutes."

John Porcelly

"Agnostic Front got a record deal with Combat Core, a subsidiary of Relativity Records, and Roger came up to me and asked if I would do a cover [for the 12"]. I asked what he wanted and he said, 'Do your version of hell.' Steve Sinclair [Combat Core A&R] said he didn't like my first drawing because 'it wasn't shocking enough.' I told him that if I did something I thought was shocking that it wouldn't get into stores. He said, 'Oh no don't worry about that. Don't tell me how to run my business. Just give me a shocking album cover and I'll do my job.' I drew another cover and everyone in Agnostic Front was happy with it. Stigma loved it. Steve saw it and said, 'Yeah that's what I mean.' Later, Steve came to me saying they couldn't use it because stores wouldn't carry it. It was too scary. This art was later used for their tour shirt."

Sean Taggart

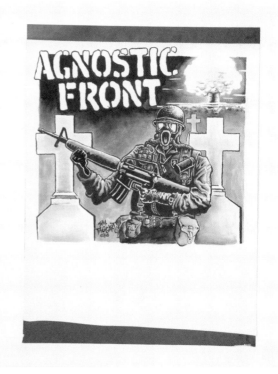

118.133 [above]
Agnostic Front *Eliminator*, 1986;
Illustration by Sean Taggart

118.134 [below]
Agnostic Front *Cause For Alarm*
12" [Combat Core/Relativity,
1986] rejected cover art;
Illustration by Sean Taggart
This artwork was deemed too
offensive by Combat Core and
was subsequently changed.

119.135 [opposite, top-bottom]
Trip Six *Back With A
Vengeance Demo* cassette;
Rat Boy Records, 1987
Bustin' Out *Demo* cassette;
Streetstyle Productions, 1987
Sick of It All *Demo* cassette;
Alleyway Style Tapes, 1986
Life's Blood *Demo* cassette, 1988
Our Gang *Uprising Demo*
cassette, 1988
Uppercut *Demo* cassette; 1988
New Breed! Tape Compilation
cassette; Urban Style Records, 1989
Occupied Territory *A Start Demo*
cassette; 1989
Citizens Arrest *Demo* cassette;
Lifetime Records, 1989
Abombanation *Demo* cassette;
1988, ABAN Music
Cro-Mags *Age of Quarrel Demo*
cassette; Cro-Mag-Non Records
& Tapes Co., 1985
Krakdown *Demo* cassette, 1987

Craig Setari

"[The guys in] Agnostic Front were lifers. Roger and Vinnie are original old-timers. The band were flag bearers for the whole New York hardcore scene. That was a serious thing. It's not like Roger and Vinnie were going to go out and get a regular job with a suit and tie. They are street guys, so it was that type of band. Those guys lived outside the system. Before I was in Agnostic Front, I remember Roger living in a van on Avenue A with a bunch of pit bulls. I'd see him and say, 'Hey Roger' and he'd be like, 'Hey kid what are you doing?' while he was making himself a sandwich in the back of the van. He'd give half the sandwich to the pit bull, and eat the other half himself. 'OK man, see you Sunday.' I'd walk off and think, 'Damn that dude is hard.' With Youth of Today, we were, like, handing out sandwiches to homeless guys, and Roger could barely even get his own sandwich."

121.136
Murphy's Law at the
Living Room, Providence,
Rhode Island, July 27, 1986;
Photograph by JJ Gonson

122.137
RKL *Keep Laughing* original
artwork, Mystic records, 1985;
Illustration by <u>Sites</u>

90%
50%
10%

K&&

Ye

R R   O   green B/g.

white Art
white Letters
white Rocks
white Rails
SKY (Blue)
sites off   mystic cgo A

ATTN. PRINTER:
IMPORTANT!

BACKGROUND   BLUE. COLOR OF DR. KNOW green
LETTERS ON PLUG IN JESUS. MAKE SURE
TO GET IN BETWEEN RAILROAD TIES. AND SKY.
STICK TO OUTSIDE LINES. E.G. SLIMY VALLEY
                                    COVER
                                    (FLOURESCENT
R.K.L. Letters AND KEEP LAUGHING{ YELLOW

DO NOT COLOR: TRAIN, RAILS, BOY, BUILDING WINDOW
   DO COLOR: GROUND BLUE

"I guess I started to lampoon some of my 'heroes' not too long after I started to get my illustrations printed. I was much younger, I think, than a lot of the punk artists that I looked up to. I never once considered myself one of their peers, but they all inspired me greatly. Unfortunately, as we all know, you can still get a large head in the microscopic hardcore community, even back then. So you can chalk up some of this cynicism being nurtured in egomaniac encounters with some of these artists and musicians. I realized really quickly that some people just didn't seem to have a sense of humor. Also, like most people who drew stuff for people, it was all in the spirit of the times, and not for the money. Who knew who would feel ripped off, do the ripping, or have the rippers getting ripped off themselves? Eventually, I learned how to draw a lot better and discovered that a lot of good material was to be found in those memories, be it the good ones and the lame ones."

Brian Walsby

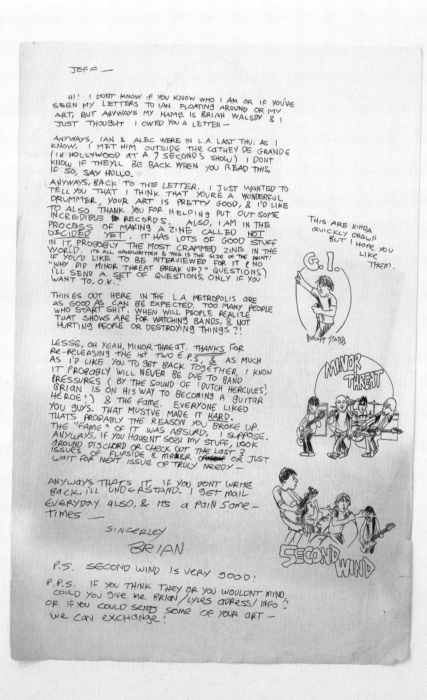

126.141 [opposite]
Hand painted **Token Entry**
denim vest, c.1986; Illustration
by Ernie Parada

127.142 [above]
Murphy's Law *Back With a Bong*
T-shirt, c.1989; Illustration by
Alex "Uncle Al" Morris

"The shows then were tiny because no one knew what hardcore was. You were a freak wherever you went. In Astoria we had this unwritten rule that if you were part of the hardcore scene you'd get on the last car on the subway. Chances are you'd see somebody you knew, and if you saw a guy wearing a Clash or Ramones shirt then you'd go up and introduce yourself. That's how we met Johnny Feedback. He was wearing a Clash shirt and we found out he was in Kraut."

Ernie Parada

"Hardcore was a cartoony experience. The cartoon drawing covers really captured what it was like because you often felt like you were trapped in a comic book."

Kevin Egan

128.143 [previous spread]
Cro-Mags at The Ritz, New York,
New York, 1986; Photograph
by JJ Gonson

130.144 [above]
Release windbreaker, c.1989;
Illustration by Chris Cap

"In the summer of 1989 Release played a show in Buffalo, New York with Zero Tolerance and we ended
up at a Champion clothing outlet. As much as Nike was the symbol of clean-cut straight edge bands
of the late '80s, I think Champion was even more of a must-have brand. A bunch of us ended up
buying these Champion windbreakers. Our drummer Chris Cap was a great artist, great in the sense
that I've never seen anyone draw a better cartoon depiction of a hooded dude with a bat, so we decided
that he should draw on the back of these jackets. The following day we played in Cleveland, Ohio
and we wore our jackets proudly."

Chris Zusi

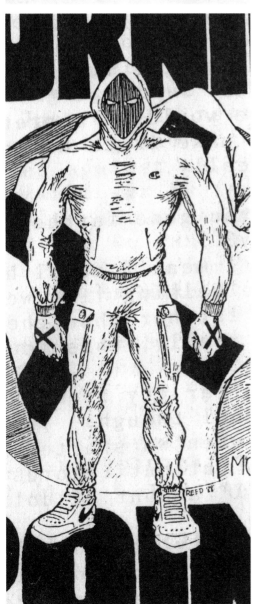

"Other than New York City bands, I don't think that there were any hardcore bands at the time getting up. Suicidal was doing gang writing, but they weren't really graffiti writers, it was just straight gang writing."

Erik Brunetti

"The first guy to really introduce hip-hop in the hardcore scene had to be the first singer of the Cro-Mags, Eric Cassanova. He would break-dance and do some popping and locking b-boy moves in between songs on stage."

Sean Taggart

"Ric Clayton brought that West L.A. gang style to Suicidal. He was an urban legend type guy from the scene who played bass for No Mercy and did a lot of gang style artwork."

Shaun Ross

132.152 [opposite above]
New Breed! *Tape Compilation*
[insert detail], Urban Style
Records, 1989

132.153 [opposite below]
Outburst *Miles to Go* 7"; Blackout!
Records, 1989; Design by <u>Bill
Wilson</u>, photograph by <u>BJ Papas</u>,
typography by <u>Jay Rufino</u>

133.154 [above]
Welcome to Venice 12"; Suicidal
Records, 1985; Illustration by
<u>Ric Clayton</u>

133.155 [below]
Sketchbook detail, 1987;
Illustration by <u>Shaun Ross</u>

and a lot more people are into us, and ③ there's not nearly as many problems

we are just bummed about all this **bullshit**, cause we're a band and we wanna play for people & we think the kind of music we play is happening. All this B.S. has left a sour taste in our mouths ~~where~~ we are bummed with a lot of Punk Rock & now we put Suicidal as our #1 priority rather than **Punk rock**. A lot of people tried to stop our band but we stuck it out, thru difficult times and B.S. lies & rumors about us, to get our album out and now a lot of those Suicidal Haters are way into us. It's still hard being Suicidal Tendencies, the band, but no ones gonna stop us because we have our integrity & pride & we know we'll end up being proven right. So Pat. don't go out looking for trouble, but when trouble comes to you, make it fucking regret it, cause your right & there wrong. You'll come out on top in the long run. **Keep up** your band, and maybe some day we'll play together. I hope you can understand this letter. If you got any questions about this or the band write back & I'll be happy to answer them. Write back and tell me if you guys have had any more problems & what, etc. & if more people are getting into us ($) from your area & where you go to gigs at, and if there's any club ~~down~~ around there that we could play at.

Thanx again & sorry for taking so long,

Mike Muir $

P.S. Yes I know Rob & Pete, they're real cool
P.S.S. $ silk screened shirts "Possessed" model cost $6 we pay postage & handling
P.S.S.S. I answer all our letters, but I try to answer them the same day I get them, which I can do now that we're back from tour, so when you write back you'll get an immediate reply... none of this B.S. Thanx!

134.156 [opposite]
Letter from Mike Muir
to Pat Dubar, 1985

135.157 [above]
Suicidal Tendencies Venice,
California, 1983; Photograph
by Glen E. Friedman
Originally published on the cover
of *Flipside* magazine #41, 1983

"The way that gangs started infiltrating hardcore was because of Jay Adams. There was an incident at Okidogs between the L.A.D.S. and Suicidals that involved Jay, Mike Muir, and Greg Graffin that started the whole thing and made people choose sides.

Punks were a minority and they became down with the Cholos, then you had Cholos turning punk. Fenders was the most violent any music scene has ever been, period. In 1986 during three songs you'd have more violence than at Altamont. The clubs would hire Samoan gangs as security guards and eventually they started claiming Suicidal, which brought gangs more towards the hardcore scene. They weren't just random security guys, they were violent Samoan crips who became part of the scene."

Shaun Ross

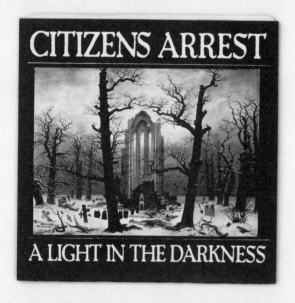

CITIZENS ARREST

A LIGHT IN THE DARKNESS

136.158 [previous spread]
Crucifix at Benny's, Richmond Virginia, June 24, 1983;
Photograph by <u>Rusty Moore</u>

138.159 [above]
Citizens Arrest *A Light In The Darkness* 7"; Wardance Records, 1990; *Cloister Cemetery in the Snow* painting by Caspar David Friedrich, c.1817–19, destroyed 1945, formerly in the National Gallery, Berlin, Germany, design by <u>Patrick Winter</u>

138.160 [above right]
Citizens Arrest *A Light In The Darkness* 7" [inside cover detail]; Wardance records, 1990; Design by <u>Patrick Winter</u>

138.161 [right]
Citizens Arrest *A Light In The Darkness* 7" [poster detail]; Wardance records, 1990; Design by <u>Patrick Winter</u>

139.162 [opposite above]
Rorschach *Needlepack* 7", production mechanical; Wardance Records, 1991; Design by <u>Melissa York</u>

139.163 [opposite below]
Rorschach *Needlepack* 7" [gatefold detail]; Wardance Records, 1991; Design by <u>Melissa York</u>

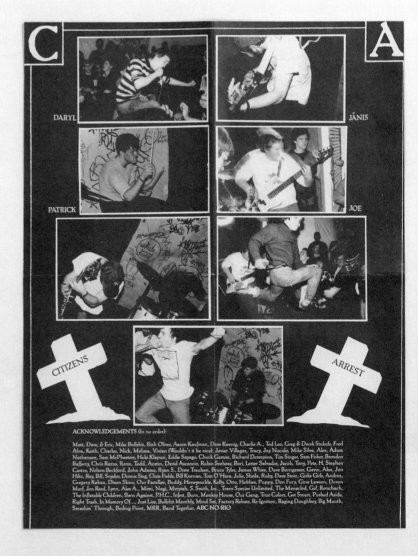

DARYL
JÁNIS
PATRICK
JOE
CITIZENS
ARREST

ACKNOWLEDGEMENTS (in no order):
Matt, Dave, & Eric, Mike Bullshit, Rich Oliver, Aaron Kaufman, Dave Koenig, Charlie A., Ted Leo, Greg & Derek Stukuls, Fred Alva, Keith, Charles, Nick, Melissa, Vivian (Wouldn't it be nice), Javier Villegas, Tracy, Jay Nocida, Mike Silva, Alex, Adam Nathanson, Sam McPheeters, Hobi Klapuri, Eddie Sayago, Chuck Gomez, Richard Derespina, Tim Singer, Sam Fisher, Brendan Rafferty, Chris Razzo, Ronn, Todd, Austin, David Ascencio, Rubin Seethner, Bari, Lester Salvador, Jacob, Tony, Pete, H. Stephen Castro, Nelson Beckford, John Adams, Ryan S., Drew Traulsen, Bruce Tyler, James White, Dave Borngesser, Gavin, Alex, Jon Hiltz, Ray, Bill, Snydor, Dennis Sieg, Chris Fields, Bill Kiernan, Tom O'Hara, Julie, Sheila, Ruby, Dave Stein, Girlie Girls, Andrea, Gregory Kahan, Dixon Skins, Our Families, Buddy, Honeysuckle, Kelly, Otto, Hobbes, Puppy, Don Fury, Gina Lawson, Devon Morf, Jon Reed, Lynn, Alex A., Mimi, Nagi, Mirjiah, S. Smith, Inc., Trans Species Unlimited, The Manacled, Go!, Rorschach, The Inflatable Children, Born Against, P.H.C., Infest, Burn, Monkey House, Our Gang, True Colors, Get Smart, Pushed Aside, Right Trash, In Memory Of..., Just Lies, Bullshit Monthly, Mind Set, Factory Rebate, Re-Ignition, Raging Doughboy, Big Mouth, Smashin' Through, Boiling Point, MRR, Band Together, ABC-NO-RIO

"Cancer put a whole new perspective on life for me. I had been listening to people sing about subjects as 'important' as scene unity, and beer drinking, and not drinking beer, and fighting each other, and friendship and vegetarianism. That shit made no sense to me. Why would I expend energy, time, and effort getting a band together to stand on a stage in front of 300 straight edge kids and say, 'This song is about straight edge' just to get a huge applause and a bunch of people jumping on stage to sing along? Nick and I wrote the lyrics and we wanted to have people read them and think. That's it, just think. Think about the shit going on around them. Think about the fact that all of this shit is happening and they 'Remain Sedate' because it is easier to just go see a band that tells them they are doing the right thing and everything will be okay. We were going back to the lyrical approach of early '80s bands like Black Flag, Dead Kennedys, and COC where there was an actual emotional connection."

Charles Maggio

140.164
Nation of Ulysses at Ocho Loco,
San Francisco, California,
August, 1992; Photograph by
Jeff Winterberg

"With Nation of Ulysses you couldn't tell if they were serious, a parody, or if they were doing a serious parody. They brought a new element of style and presentation, referencing the dress of bands like the Jam but in a new way and context. What was brilliant about them was that they were a goof on pop culture, underground culture, and everything."

Kevin Egan

142.165
Ulysses Speaks fanzine #00-008;
c.1990; Published by the
Nation of Ulysses

"Nobody really believed that Nation of Ulysses were
a terrorist group, but the *Ulysses Speaks* 'zines really
created another mystery around the band. This was
the first 'zine I saw that was intentionally confusing.
I wrote a letter asking for a T-shirt and they replied
'We don't sell T-shirts, only armaments.'"

Jeff Winterberg

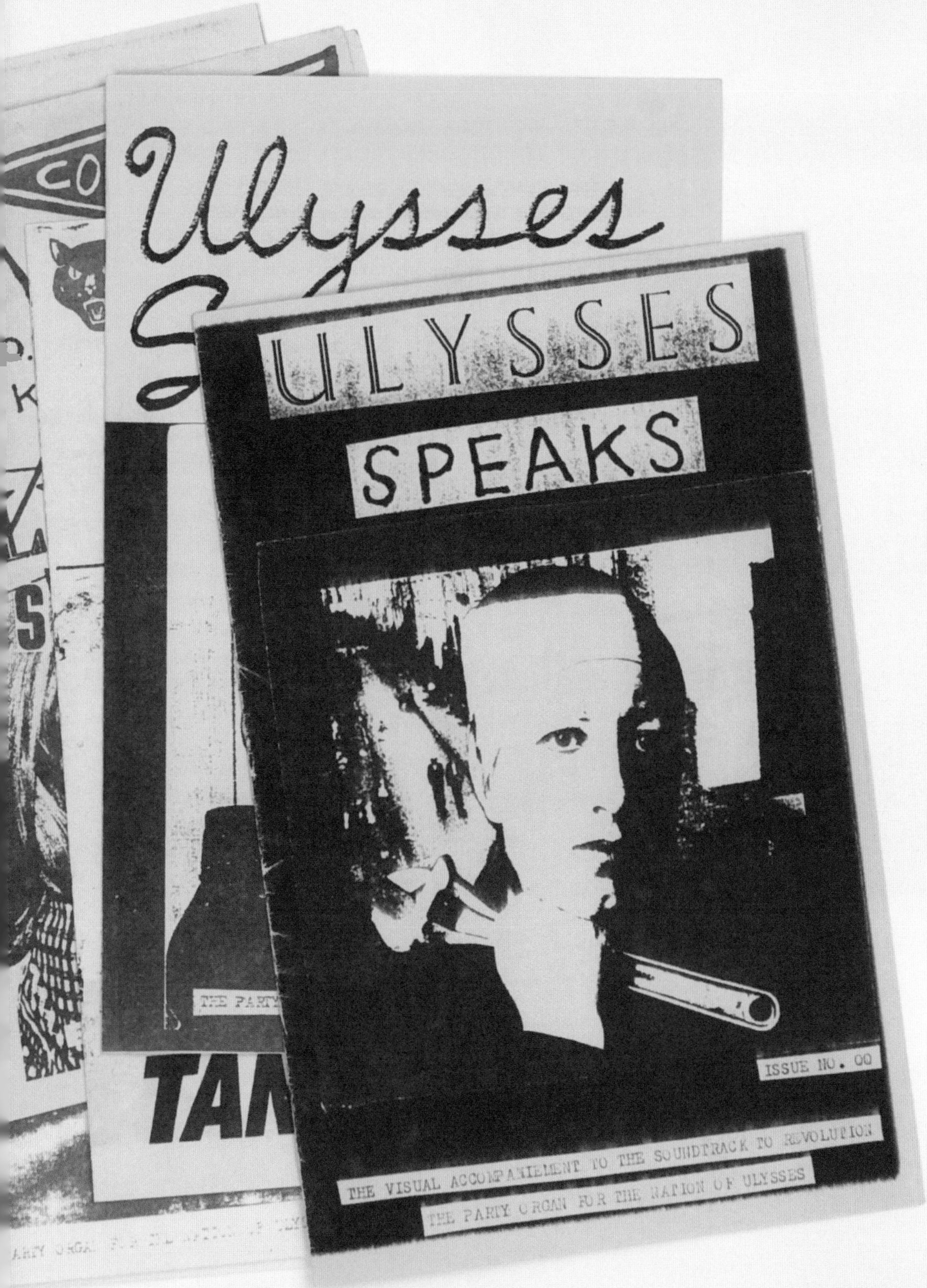

CO

Ulysses S

P.
K

TAN

ULYSSES
SPEAKS

ISSUE NO. 00

THE VISUAL ACCOMPANIEMENT TO THE SOUNDTRACK TO REVOLUTION
THE PARTY ORGAN FOR THE NATION OF ULYSSES

144.166 [above]
Clikatat Ikatowi at 915 E Street.
San Diego, California. May, 1993;
Photograph by Jeff Winterberg

144.167 [right]
Moss Icon/Silver Bearing
split 12"; Vermin Scum, 1991;
Design by Tonie Joy

145.168 [opposite]
Drive Like Jehu at the
Casbah, San Diego, California.
August 2, 1992; Photograph
by Jeff Winterberg

"In California in the late '80s, if you were in a band playing a club that served alcohol, and you were under 21 you would literally have to go from the stage to the door after doing your sound check. You were not allowed in the club if alcohol was being served. You couldn't even walk around the club or watch other bands. The Ché Café, and all the garage shows would happen just so you could even have all ages shows. There was a point where the Ché was closed down and we used to sneak into the basement of the UCSD library where they had these rehearsal spaces that weren't locked up and seldom patrolled so we would book shows and even have dance parties there."

Jeff Winterberg

"We were just poor but even if we had tons of cash our records would still have been an artistic effort or expression, not some glossy lifeless bullshit. To us our records were more meaningful than just a product. There was a connection subculturally, socially, and spiritually. It was like a craft, grassroots, cottage industry thing. We were just plopped down into the macho scene like aliens crash landing and having to deal with the inhabitants of where we ended up. It's just random chance that we worked in that network [hardcore] playing shows. We just wanted to play to humans [preferably young] so in that day and age we ended up at those shows with that audience."

Tonie Joy

Thread

Tap and Die

Time Without

A Cry for Truth

Escape

Exit

DOWN SIDE · VINYL COMMUNICATIONS
P.O. Box 8623, Chula Vista, CA 92012

"Amenity was a really important band that kept hardcore alive in San Diego for a younger generation. They bridged the gap between the old school violent scene and the '90s scene. Amenity helped shape San Diego in a really positive way along with Pitchfork, Neighborhood Watch, and Vinyl Communications. *This is Our Struggle* was an anthem at the Ché Café, and anywhere else Amenity played. Mike Down was very influential on Gravity records graphically with the stamped art and textured paper. He knew how important packaging was. In the '80s just having a record out was amazing enough, but in the '90s the next step was to make the packaging more personal and creative."

Matt Anderson

"The [Amenity] artwork was done by our guitar player, Tim Gonzales. It was making a statement about borders and our scene and looking at it from a different angle. The T-shirt art was the Chula Vista community logo that we just slapped on a shirt.

We wanted everything to look expensive, but we were pressing very limited quantities, and had no budget. We would hang out at the paper suppliers and get deals and free paper on some of their newer stocks that they were promoting. We would just have the black ink off-set printed, then had custom stamps made for like 10 bucks. Everyone would come over and we would stamp the colors on the paper. It was like a production line with people folding covers. As our arms got tired some of the stamping would go crazy, so every cover was unique. Recently I had the original artwork for the *Forced Down* 7" framed. When it was done, I realized that it cost more than the entire budget for the recording, pressing, and printing of the actual record.

We never had any background in art or design. A lot of the typesetting was done with those old rub-off letters. We would spend nights on end doing layouts with rulers, glue sticks, and blue line photo boards lining up everything by hand. When I think of the hours it took to get the package how we wanted it… it's crazy. A weeks worth of work then can now be done in literally a few hours."

<u>Mike Down</u>

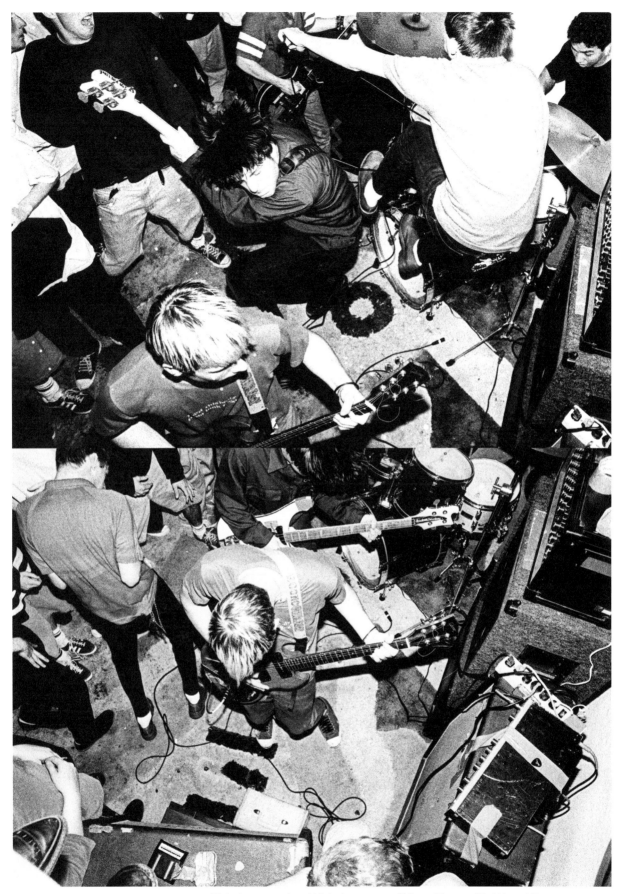

148.175, 148.176,
148.177, 148.178
Antioch Arrow at 915 E. Street.
San Diego, California. May, 1993;
Photograph by Cameron Campbell
[using Jeff Winterberg's camera]

"Only about 20 people could fit in the room at 915 E. Street. The rest of the kids would have to pile up on the wall behind the drummer or on the wall facing it. We had just watched *The Kids Are Alright* and Aaron was swinging the mic around like Roger Daltrey but he was so close to everyone that he was completely knocking everyone in the head."

Jeff Winterberg

150.179 [above]
Heroin at ABC No Rio, New
York, New York, 1993; Photograph
by Glenn Maryansky

151.180 [opposite above]
Heroin s/t 12";
Vermiform records, 1994
*The reason we made the limited
edition cover is because the real
covers weren't done in time for
our U.S. tour. We made these so
we could have records for the tour.
It was pretty much the same art as
the normal 12". I got the art out of
a book at a library about anatomy
and fossils.* —MATT ANDERSON

151.181 [opposite below]
Heroin T-shirt, c.1993; Illustration
by Matt Anderson, screen printed
by Crisanta Nucci

"We [Heroin] never made T-shirts ourselves but our friend Crisanta Nucci made some and would
sell them at shows. I got the artwork from a skate 'zine, but I changed the cross to a gun, with the
cross in the reflection. All of the shirts were done on thrift store shirts with water-based inks. You
just have to make sure you put them in the dryer before you wash them.

I was really excited to play at ABC No Rio. We played downstairs. That whole day I was walking
around New York with no shoes because the night before we got jumped at a Taco Bell in Philadelphia.
We had walked back into the drive-through to get more hot sauce and these guys in line jumped out
of their car and started smashing in the windows of our van. They punched our bass player, and my
shoes came off as one of the guys tried to pull me out of the van. A nice guy at ABC No Rio gave
me some old boots."

Matt Anderson

"Antioch Arrow never actually played with Heroin even though we shared a member. We had a lot of
weird rules, like you couldn't wear shorts, and no shirts off while playing. It was tongue-in-cheek but
there was a level of seriousness too. Tons of hardcore dudes would take their shirts off at shows, and
I guess it was somewhat a reaction to that whole thing. Ron used to have a horrible rack system that
he used for his drums and we asked him to get rid of it because it looked so ridiculous."

Jeff Winterberg

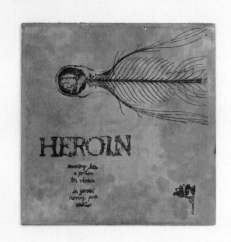

152.182 [above]
Downcast at the Red Barn,
Santa Barbara, California, 1990;
Photograph by
David "Igby" Sattanni

152.183 [right]
Econochrist at Cell 63, Simi Valley,
1992; Photograph by Dave Sine

153.184 [opposite]
Born Against outside Spanky's
Cafe, Riverside, California, July 7,
1991; Photograph by Dave Sine
*I don't know the details, but when
I arrived the bands decided to play
outside in front of Spanky's instead in
the venue. They found power in the
light poles and used a bass amp for
the P.A. Sam wasn't around, so Born
Against just played an instrumental
set. Surprisingly, the cops never
showed up.* — DAVE SINE

"I loved playing small shows in intimate
settings. I loved feeling like I could
connect with a majority of people in the
room. I also loved playing big shows
and being able to ruffle feathers, and
make people think. Every big show
Rorschach played was the result of
some headlining band. People had to
see us in order to see the band they
came to see but when we played the
living room of a house in Amarillo,
Texas for 15 people and we were the
headliner, people were there because
they wanted to see us, and it felt good
that 15 people cared. To me it felt better
to play for 15 people that cared than
500 that didn't. As a band we certainly
wanted to grow an audience and get
bigger, but I was very conscious of the
price we would be paying to do so. It
eventually tore the band apart."

Charles Maggio

"Born Against and Rorschach played outside in front of the club in protest of the club's door price, for the show we were supposed to have done inside that afternoon. It was fun to play outside spontaneously in a public square setting, but our reasons for doing so were kind of stupid. We took such a strong stance against door prices above five dollars, and as I recall, this one was around eight dollars. Whatever. The middle aged Middle Eastern guy who ran the club was totally confused. He had a reputation for ripping off the bands, but in the long run, who cares?"

Adam Nathanson

154.185 [above]
Born Against at Toe Jam, Long
Beach, California, February, 1993;
Photograph by <u>Dave Sine</u>

155.186 [opposite]
Rorschach outside Spanky's,
Riverside, California, July 7th, 1991;
Photograph by <u>Dave Sine</u>

156.187 [above left]
Los Crudos *Las Injusticias Caen Como Pesadillas* 7", Leguna Armada Records, 1993; Design by Martin Sorrondeguy

156.188 [above right]
Los Crudos *Las Injusticias Caen Como Pesadillas* 7" [insert detail], Leguna Armada Records, 1993; Design by Martin Sorrondeguy

156.189 [right]
Spitboy Santa Barbara, California, 1992; Photograph by Dave Sine

157.190 [opposite above]
Universal Order of Armageddon at Macondo, Los Angeles, California. October 1993; Photograph by Jeff Winterberg

157.191 [opposite below]
Universal Order of Armageddon *Demo*; Vermin Scum Records, 1992

"The 169 House was sort of the Ché
Café of Annapolis, Maryland. It was this
big house in the suburbs of Annapolis,
Maryland that completely didn't fit in.
There was a rotating cast of about
twenty people who paid about three
hundred dollars a month in rent. They
had a spacious basement where they
could have shows. Every band who was
in that loop stayed there and played
there. Universal Order of Armageddon
practiced there, and it was just generally
some stinky punk house plopped
into the middle of an otherwise quiet
neighborhood. Antioch Arrow only
did one show there but we used it as a
base of operations for about a week of
tour. We'd go play Washington, D.C.
and come back to sleep there instead
of staying in town. I heard secondhand
that the D.C. kids were buzzing about
how we came and played St Stephen's,
played a totally insane set, and then
disappeared. We only disappeared
because we felt more comfortable
going back to 169 in Annapolis."

Jeff Winterberg

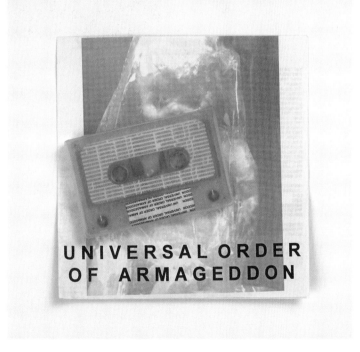

UNIVERSAL ORDER
OF ARMAGEDDON

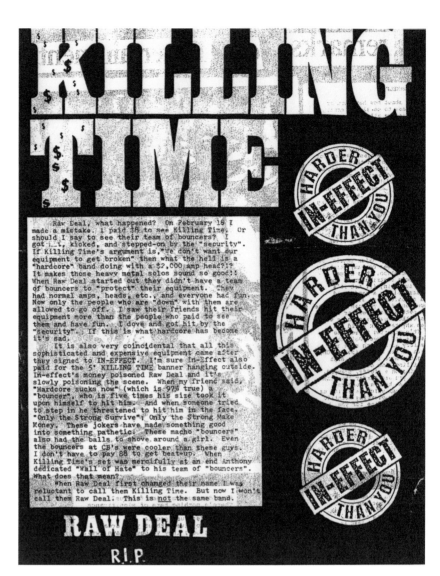

"I went to the NYU debate [between Sick of It All and Born Against] because the Sick of It All guys asked me to go with them. Sick of It All was upset that the guys from Born Against had just flyered a show they played at The Ritz. The issue was that we [Sick of It All and Agnostic Front] played big shows with big promoters, but we explained that both bands played bigger shows because we drew bigger crowds, but that we also went back and played CBGB whenever we could, because we hadn't abandoned that ideal. The people they were bad-mouthing, Agnostic Front, Cro-Mags and Sick of It All, had built the roads these guys were traveling on, and they chose to expand their fan base by doing attack ads on bigger bands. Sick of It All, Agnostic Front, Cro-Mags, these were working class and lower class guys who had no other alternative. They had to survive by touring and selling records. To begrudge them for taking a bigger guarantee to play for more fans was terrible. Vermiform and In-Effect had the same distributor, Important Records. The only difference was that In-Effect had a staff and a warehouse in a shitty neighborhood in Queens. Vermiform was just branding themselves differently."

Steve Martin

"When In-Effect came in it made things feel legitimate. It was like 'sign a paper and we'll give you enough money to eat what you want, and your record will come out.' With Agnostic Front it was, 'let's play, let's do this,' There was no long term plan, it was all moving so fast. We didn't realize there was an opportunity there. I don't know what the opportunity really was, maybe to be legitimate to a bunch of people that you never wanted to be legitimate to anyway. Anything an 'adult person' would think was legitimate meant nothing to me, and when I say an 'adult person,' I half mean asshole."

Craig Setari

"CBGB had gotten so violent, that they stopped doing hardcore shows for a while. People were getting stabbed and guns were being confiscated. All the people going to CBGB to flex their muscles, swing chains, pick fights, and do flying axe kicks around the pit no longer had a place to go. They seemingly shrugged their shoulders and faded away. Those of us who were in the back, trying not to make eye contact with those people, and survive another Sunday there without getting hurt just to be able to see the bands and the music that we loved so much, were left out in the cold with nothing but the desire to see it go on. Those people—the ones with the passion and love for the music—decided that a new place needed to happen, but it needed to be done with a new set of rules. Rules that protected us, and kept us safe while still being able to enjoy the music."

Charles Maggio

"There were a lot of people who thought the big business infiltration of hardcore was fucked up, and they were making it known in 'zines, on stage, and on flyers; and I got caught up in it. Thinking Killing Time was responsible for what was going on, I let some people convince me to make a flyer about it, and hand it out at a Swiz show in New York City. It took about ten minutes before Drago, Killing Time's drummer, got wind of the flyer and was at the show looking to kill someone. Luckily for me, my friends intercepted him at the door while I was watching Swiz. Later that night I got a call telling me to 'have my shit together because Tony's going to kill you.' Two weeks later Killing Time were playing at the Anthrax in Connecticut and I felt compelled to go; they were my favorite band after all. Tony gets up on stage with a Dokken poster, screaming into the mic. 'People are saying that we've gone metal! Well, this is fucking metal [holds up the poster] and we're not a fucking metal band!' And he tears the thing to shreds over the bass line to 'New Release.' Making that flyer had to be the dumbest thing I ever did."

Brett Beach

Why do I always have to spell it out for you? /
Our story is always changing.

Quicksand "Omission"

"With Quicksand I was trying to take that energy of hardcore and apply it to something new by using different musicians from different backgrounds. I wanted to create something that was the next step of hardcore by connecting hardcore's energy with hip-hop. I was into what Public Enemy were doing, and I was listening to Slayer a lot. It made sense to us, and we also mixed in some Sub Pop stuff like Soundgarden. I didn't see it as having any commercial appeal. When the major label thing happened I wasn't that into it. I thought we would pretty much fail on a major, but I was 21 and it was a chance to do something fun and exciting. I wasn't even into the original sound by the time we made the album. I thought the music that the band was influenced by originally was stupid. I was getting into shoegaze and My Bloody Valentine. Me, Serge, and Tom would buy every Creation single, anything tangent to that scene. We brought that into what we were doing. With *Slip* I felt sad that once it was done we were going to be in the category of a 'rock band' because in my heart I was into something totally different."

Walter Schreifels

"I got into underground stuff early on through reading about Charles Manson and industrial music like Psychic TV. I was really into Current 93, I would play a show with Quicksand and meet up with David Tibet later. Drew Thomas and I became really tight when I joined Bold, and we were both into the occult. We would read books [about the occult] and do rituals. Most people were freaked out by it, or didn't understand it. Walter always thought the satanic stuff was really funny. In 1989 on the Bold and Gorilla Biscuits summer tour the Gorilla Biscuits van caught up to the Bold van and they all saw me reading a book called *Satan Wants You*. They thought I was some crazy devil worshipper. The name Quicksand actually came from a David Bowie song called "Quicksand" where he talks about Aleister Crowley."

Tom Capone

162.195 [previous spread]
Supertouch, Queens, New York, 1990; Out take from the *The Earth Is Flat* 12" cover shoot [Revelation Records, 1990]; Photograph by Theresa Kelliher
Mark Ryan was my roommate at the time and we were sharing a studio with another person [three of us in a studio, in true NYC-youngun form]. Someone picked us up at, like, 4:30 in the morning to drive all the way out to the Rockaways and shoot the cover.
—THERESA KELLIHER

163.196 [below]
Quicksand *s/t* 7"; Revelation Records, 1990; Designed by Jordan Cooper and Alex Brown

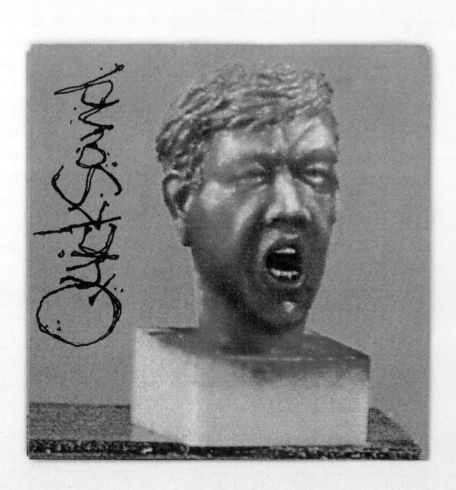

165.197 [above]
Quicksand at The Moon,
New Haven, Connecticut; 1993;
Photograph by <u>Adam Tanner</u>.
This show was set up by Fernando
Pinto who would later open up the
Tune Inn. The Moon was notorious
because there were always brawls
with the bouncers that would
inevitably end the shows early.
— ADAM TANNER

165.198 [left]
Quicksand at CBGB, New York,
New York, September, 1994;
Photograph by <u>Adam Tanner</u>.

"Kingpin began with a harder sound that was pretty typical of the Boston and New York bands at the time. We quickly realized that if we stuck with that approach it was going to be a dead end. That's when we began to add melodic elements that transformed our sound completely. The band was only together for three years, so I'm amazed when I think of all the ground we covered in such a short period of time.

One of the things that sticks out the most for me about that time is how bands were trying to explore the possibilities of what hardcore could be without submitting to clichés. A lot of people think hardcore from the early '90s sounds dated, and perhaps some of it does, but one thing you can't say about Kingpin, Eye for an Eye, or Arise is that any of us were following any rules or formulas."

Matt Kattman

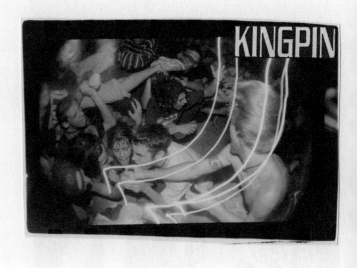

"Everyone was doing post-hardcore in the early '90s but in a lot of ways I don't think people related to what we [Into Another] were trying to communicate. I do think that kids appreciate Into Another because we were being punk. Not by dressing up as punks, but by being open and doing what we wanted to do. I wore some pretty stupid and crazy shit, but it was fun. People were really critical of how we looked. Now you have emo kids with tight black jeans and haircuts and that's a whole scene. When the early Into Another pictures were taken, Oasis still wasn't even out so it was a different landscape. That attitude of making things more open was at the helm of developing the next wave."

Drew Thomas

"Swiz, Statue, Girls Against Boys, and The Nation of Ulysses were what I refer to as 'spy rock' or 'conspiracy core.' All these bands had a cinematic flair with movies, books, and ancient jazz ideals fueling the delivery and presentation. Statue didn't actively listen to jazz, we were just fascinated by our take on what we thought Miles Davis would sound like in our hands. Statue's suits were inspired by jazz saxophone player Dexter Gordon, Echo & The Bunnymen, *London Calling*-era Mick Jones, Madness, and The Specials. I used to actually say 'look like Madness, play like Zeppelin…'"

Chris Bratton

166.199 [opposite above]
Into Another at Maxwell's, Hoboken, New Jersey, 1992; Photograph by Glenn Maryansky

167.200 [opposite below]
Kingpin [their last show] at QVCC, Worcester, Massachusetts, August 14, 1993; Photograph by Glenn Maryansky
The logo was pasted on for a layout in my fanzine — GLENN MARYANSKY

166.201 [right]
Statue at Spanky's Riverside, California, February 1991; Photograph by Ron Vickers

188.202 [below]
Strife at the Showcase Theater,
Corona, California, July 28, 1995;
Photograph by <u>David "Igby" Sattanni</u>

189.203 [opposite]
Mouthpiece at the Lost Horizon
Syracuse, New York, August 18, 1991;
Photograph by <u>Lenny Zimkus</u>

"The beginning of the '90s was rebuilding. At the tail end of the '80s it wasn't that remarkable if a show went well, GBH would fly to California to play to 3,000 people. Shows got smaller when I got into straight edge bands. I saw Insted played with some random bands like MDC and DI, but when straight edge bands started playing exclusive straight edge shows it was like starting over from scratch. When a lot of bigger bands from the late '80s were starting to wind down it always felt like something was dying for them, but I felt like something was just starting. It's not gonna be hooded sweatshirts and Air Jordans but there was something brewing. Some people in the older generation might have thought that it was over and it was time to check out, but they checked out at the wrong time. [In the early '90s] We'd see bands play to twenty people in a basement but it would be a fun show because we were part of something new."

Dave Mandell

"Unfortunately the majority of the straight edge kids of the late '80s were all going away to college in the early '90s and taking more of an interest in beer bongs and frat parties than stage diving and straight edge hardcore. Mouthpiece's first West Coast trip was in the winter of 1991. We flew out to California with Resurrection, and played a few huge shows, one being at the Roxy in Hollywood with Outspoken, A Chorus of Disapproval, Strife, and Ressurection. That show was insane, probably close to 1,000 kids in attendance. After that first California trip Strife came out East and did a short tour with us. I could definitely feel the momentum picking up."

Tim McMahon

I've started school. I've got- Philosophy, Sociology and Pschology. Pretty cool classes. Yeah others have told me that Intensity suck too. I've never heard them though so I can't pass any judgement. I hope Raw Deal / Killing Time hasn't gone metal- that would really blow. Do you have addresses for the following so I can contact them to buy Victory stuff

→ BERT'S in Deleware

CHAOS in Pennsylvania

The Victory ½ page is in this month's MRR, came out Sept 15, thus the October ish! OK. BUSINESS TIME. Right now Hi Impact looks like who we're gonna go with. They want the 7" out by X-Mas and here is what they'll give us -

$200⁰⁰ Recording time MINIMUM

FIRST 1,000 7"s pressed we get ⎱ 800 black
⎰ 200 colored

100 black
100 colored

EACH additional 1,000

100 records

2 color fold out cover

SHIRTS

Short sleeve ——→ we can get for $4
longsleeve ——→ " " " " $5   ⎫ then we turn
possibly- hats → possibly $4   ⎬ around and sell
                                      ⎭ for double the
                                         amount

If you could beat their offer we'd do Hi Impact. Get back to me ASAP, because we're very close to getting this on the move. If you could call that would be cool because then I'd be able to tell Tim Owen what's up. His deal is pretty fair I think. Also, we don't necessarily want foldout

"The first Dayton, Ohio More Than Music Festival in 1992 was Earth Crisis' first big show out of town, their "breakout" show so to speak. I had just released the *All Out War* 7" shortly before and didn't have a grasp of how popular it had become in such a short time. We got there and every 'zine had an Earth Crisis interview, photos of them or a record review. They started their set with 'Firestorm' and the place exploded. Camera flashes were going off like firecrackers. I had a video of it and we counted how many flashes went off just during that first song and it was 327 or something ridiculous. Signing to Victory was an excellent move for them. Whatever bad things we can say about the modern Victory Records, in the early '90s it was where you wanted to be, Tony pushed them hard and made it happen for them. They were promoted well, toured around the world a few times, sold a ton of records, played huge shows, changed the face and sound of hardcore and started an international movement. What more could a band want to accomplish?"

Guav

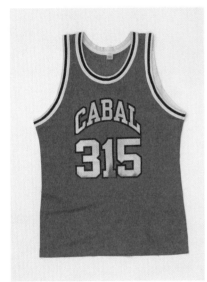

170.204 [opposite]
Letter from Tony Brummel to Darren Walters, 1989; Courtesy of Darren Walters

171.205 [above right]
Original **Earth Crisis** logotype for the *All Out War* 7", 1992; Typography by Guav
I wanted something that looked hardcore with bold lettering, but had a harder, meaner edge without looking metal. I created the basic lettering in Typestyler [early Mac program] and then drew the jagged outline with a Sanford Vis-à-Vis pen. — GUAV

171.206 [left]
Earth Crisis at Dennison Hall, Framingham, Massachusetts summer, 1993; Photograph by Adam Tanner

171.207 [above left]
Cabal 315 basketball jersey, 1994; Design by Guav

172.208
Snapcase at Limelight, New
York, New York; September, 1994;
Photograph by <u>Dave Spataro</u>

On To Greener Pastures /
Minor Threat's "Salad Days" 7"

Mark Owens

The past several years have seen a parallel rise of interest both in the history of graphic design and the music of the postpunk era. Every few months, it seems, a new book or documentary appears chronicling the contributions of an important design pioneer, influential band, or groundbreaking label.[01]

These efforts are no doubt much needed, especially given the rapid de-materialization of our popular culture into digital file formats and screen-based media. But with all of this looking back it seems worth considering what is at stake in the writing of such histories. Surely some are motivated by a simple desire to document and preserve, while others are more interested in setting the record straight or staking out neglected historical terrain. Regardless, any retrospective account inevitably stumbles on the inescapable gap between "now" and "then."

As a meditation on the recently-past heyday of early-80s hardcore, Minor Threat's *Salad Days* 7" raises all of these questions even as it stands as a landmark instance of the intersection of the history of graphic design and American postpunk. As an iconic piece of hardcore design—known to every scene veteran and budding skate punk— *Salad Days* is so familiar as to be almost invisible. Because we've long since stopped looking at it, from our present moment nearly twenty-five years on it is sometimes difficult to appreciate the excitement of what it was like to encounter *Salad Days* upon its initial release in April 1985. I was fourteen-years-old and had only recently emerged into independent musical consciousness from the clutches of MTV, radio rock, and the likes of Journey, Cheap Trick, and Hall & Oates.

Like many teenagers at the time, it was thanks to skateboarding and *Thrasher* magazine—whose absurdly cheap annual subscription came with a free Skate Rock compilation— that I was introduced to the mysterious world of punk and hardcore. Inevitably, however, my peers and I in suburban Texas were late arrivals. By the spring of 1985 the first phase of hardcore was long over, and the rumblings of Washington D.C.'s own Revolution Summer and the birth pangs of post-hardcore lay just on the horizon. Consequently, for those of us encountering it upon its release in the mid-80s *Salad Days* served a peculiar double function, both as a window into the recent past of hardcore's founding moments and as a guidepost and signal of things to come.

A crucial part of this was not only how the record itself sounded, but the way its packaging managed to capture and condense hardcore both as an aesthetic category and mode of production. In contrast to the bulk of early punk records, with their riotous cut-and-paste graphics, the cover of the *Salad Days* 7" is a minimalist tour de force, featuring only Glen E. Friedman's now-iconic black-and-white portrait of Minor Threat sitting on the steps of the Dischord House. At the time it was a dramatic gesture, a fitting final bow for one of the scene's most important bands. But for teenagers like me the cover prompted another important realization: these guys looked like us. Whereas first wave punks were characterized by their outrageous fashions, hardcore had signaled a dramatic stylistic shift.

Indeed, circa 1980 early D.C. hardcore bands like the Teen Idles had mimicked

174.209 [opposite]
Original sketch for the **Minor Threat** *Salad Days* 7", 1985.
Illustration by Jeff Nelson

176.220 [following spread]
Original contact sheet with photographers selects for the **Minor Threat** *Salad Days* 7", 1983.
Photograph by Glen E. Friedman

British punk styles, wearing safety pins, leather jackets, combat boots and the like. But soon, after a couple of years of dressing to intimidate those outside the scene (and to impress those within it), D.C. punks tired of dressing up and opted instead for street clothes and everyday fashions. On the *Salad Days* cover singer Ian MacKaye sits front-and-center wearing a T-shirt, shorts, and low-top Vans, the skateboarder's outfit of choice, and bassist Brian Baker sports Nikes, jeans, and a hooded sweatshirt, a look that would later become a kind of hardcore uniform. Meanwhile, drummer Jeff Nelson and guitarist Lyle Preslar wear jeans and button-down shirts, looking as if they'd just arrived from a student council meeting.

This dressed-down aesthetic was both a sign of hardcore's rejection of first-wave punk's nihilism and showboating, and a crucial component of its inclusiveness and ability to rupture the surface of middle-class bourgeois normality. That such alien, aggressive music—played at breakneck speed and with screamed vocals laced with profanity—could be made by seemingly average kids was both an affront to Reagan-era values and evidence of the discontent bubbling just beneath the surface in suburban homes across America. For many U.S. teenagers in the mid-80s, hardcore reached them both after-the-fact and just-in-time. As an indigenous musical idiom for the expression of alienation, anger, politics, and rebellion, hardcore offered the perfect antidote to conformist preppy fashions and the overblown production values of mainstream rock.

Perhaps more than any other record, *Salad Days* thus served as a primer not only for how hardcore sounded and looked, but how it could be done. Scrutinized with an almost Talmudic attention to detail, the photos on the lyric sheet insert to the *Salad Days* 7" offered not only an image of the band on stage, but an important glimpse behind-the-scenes. Only Brian Baker is shown playing live, while Ian MacKaye is pictured smiling, kneeling at the front of the stage engaging with audience members. Lyle Preslar, meanwhile, is photographed practicing in the Dischord House basement, bent forward because of the low ceiling and wearing a jacket against the cold. Finally, Jeff Nelson is pictured, not playing the drums, but creating the layout for Minor Threat's landmark *Out of Step* 12", released almost exactly two years before *Salad Days*.

The importance of this last photograph for a whole generation of graphic designers weaned on punk and hardcore cannot be overstated. Taken by D.C. photographer and designer Cynthia Connolly, whose original illustration appears on the cover of

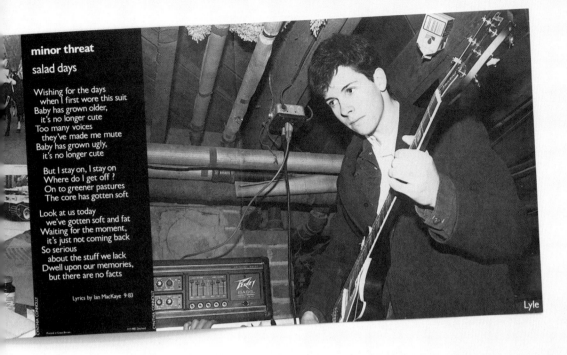

minor threat

salad days

Wishing for the days
  when I first wore this suit
Baby has grown older,
  it's no longer cute
Too many voices
  they've made me mute
Baby has grown ugly,
  it's no longer cute

But I stay on, I stay on
Where do I get off ?
On to greener pastures
The core has gotten soft

Look at us today
  we've gotten soft and fat
Waiting for the moment,
  it's just not coming back
So serious
  about the stuff we lack
Dwell upon our memories,
  but there are no facts

Lyrics by Ian MacKaye 9-83

Lyle

Out of Step, the photograph shows Nelson, type-burnisher in hand, with the now familiar typography, Minor Threat logo, and jumping sheep graphic spread out on the plywood lap desk before him, a bottle of rubber cement and sheets of rubdown lettering by his side. While the example of groups like Bad Brains and Black Flag had encouraged countless teenagers to pick up instruments and start bands, this photograph similarly opened up the tools of graphic design to scores of non-professionals whose logos, T-shirts, and record covers would go on to form the visual language of hardcore, post-hardcore, and indie rock well into the next decade.

Certainly, by the mid-80s the DIY media of punk 'zines, show flyers, T-shirts, record covers, and other printed matter was nothing new. But the actual material process of design was perhaps never before so explicitly visualized within the continuum of creative production that constituted participation in the hardcore scene as in the *Salad Days* 7". As a founding instance of hardcore design, *Out of Step* had itself quickly become something of an iconic artifact, thanks in large part to the fact that it had been released shortly before Minor Threat had broken up, but just as the band was gaining widespread national attention in the underground. Indeed, for anyone who had come to hardcore after 1983 (which was the bulk of the rapidly growing scene), Minor Threat was already a legendary group that was only ever available through their records, mix tapes, photographs in fanzines, and the occasional grainy videotape.

As if to underscore this fact, the highly sought after first pressing of *Out of Step* had appeared with a somber, stark black back cover—no photographs, no song titles, and no label information. As it happens, this was not a deliberate design decision, but rather the result of Nelson's incorrect application of a dot screen tint to the original layout. Unable to correct the camera-ready artwork, the printer had simply opted to run the entire back cover solid black.[02] For those who mourned Minor Threat's break-up, having never seen the band live, the black back cover of *Out of Step* seemed entirely appropriate and only increased the mystique and sense of insider knowledge associated with hardcore. As I've argued elsewhere, this tendency to withhold information and to suspend authorship through pseudonyms, strategic anonymity, and graphic abstraction was a crucial component of hardcore's disseminative logic, tactics it shared with the early modernist avant gardes.[03]

178.211 [above]
Minor Threat *Salad Days* insert, 1985; Design by Jeff Nelson

178.212 [opposite below]
Skate Rock Vol. 02, *Blazing Wheels and Barking Trucks. Thrasher* magazine/High Speed Productions, 1984

Looking back, hardcore graphics' formal connections with early modernism are not hard to discern, particularly its penchant for bold typography, high-contrast photographs, thick lines, and abstract geometric forms. But unlike British postpunk's savvy, art school quotationalism, such moves were largely the products of naïve necessity and limited access to graphic tools that were affordable, easily available, and ready-at-hand. Xerography, rub-down transfer lettering, pen-and-ink, and black-and-white photography: these were the raw materials from which hardcore designers sought to visualize the scene's music and ethos. As can be seen in Nelson's earliest singles for Dischord, in its formative years hardcore graphics were largely indebted to '77 punk precedents. Notably, the Teen Idles and Dischord logos were both greatly inspired by one of Nelson's favorite groups, pioneering Aussie punk band The Saints.[04]

Still, by 1981 the outlines of a recognizable hardcore graphic aesthetic had begun to emerge, particularly in Nelson's designs for Minor Threat's first two 7"s and Dischord's *Flex Your Head* compilation. Here, the favored typeface was Franklin Gothic Condensed, one of the most widely available rub-down fonts. But rather than mimic Jamie Reid's playful ransom note typography or British postpunk's studied neoclassicism, Nelson approached Franklin Gothic with a measured degree of control and pragmatism. Tightly kerned and typeset by hand for clarity, impact, and sheer density of information, Nelson's typography perfectly captured the music's blunt, no-nonsense approach and rowdy urgency. Crammed with song titles, thank-yous, credits, pricing and label information, these releases everywhere announce their embeddedness in a vibrant, highly collaborative creative community.

Indeed, over the course of 1981 and 1982 national distribution of Dischord's releases and touring by the recently re-formed Minor Threat had brought widespread attention to the D.C. scene, connecting it with a network of allied bands across North America. A corresponding explosion of creative output followed, with local and regional labels offering their own take on hardcore music and graphics.[05] In the meantime, Nelson refined his command of the tools at his disposal and began to consolidate a more designerly approach to his work for Dischord's records and ads, incorporating serif fonts, boxes, rules, spot colors, and halftone screens. His back cover design for Minor Threat's *Out of Step* 12" [see 035.033]—finally corrected in its second pressing—shows all the signs of this new level of refinement and signaled Dischord's move toward an increasingly sophisticated, coherent look for its releases.

The product of experience as much as anything else, this change signaled a gradual shift in the hardcore scene at large. As early as 1983 divisions had begun to splinter the tight-knit community. In particular, the dogmatic interpretation of Minor Threat's

chartpak Velvet Touch Lettering
franklin gothic cond. 60PT/M1160C
chartpak Velvet Touch Lettering
franklin gothic cond. 60PT/M1160C

minor threat

salad days
stumped
good guys

recorded 12·14·83
at inner ear studios.
engineer · don zientara
mix · jeff, lyle, don
photos · back · tomas
front · glen e. friedman
art · jeff nelson
dischord fifteen

℗© 1985 Dischord
Printed in France

DISCHORD
records

3819 beecher st. nw, washington, dc. 20007

182.216 [above]
Minor Threat *Salad Days* 7" [back cover detail], Dischord Records, 1985; Photograph by Tomas Squip

183.217 [opposite above]
State of the Union compilation 12". Dischord Records, 1989; Cover photograph by Jim Hubbard

183.218 [opposite above]
Original blueline artboards for the **Minor Threat** *Salad Days* insert, 1985; Typography by Jeff Nelson

song "Straight Edge" by a number of bands, and the increasing violence at shows had become tiresome and frustrating for those who had initially been drawn to hardcore for its inclusiveness and progressive politics. Similarly, as the musicians themselves began to master their instruments a number of hardcore bands turned inward, moving in an increasingly commercial, metal-influenced direction, while others began to look outside the scene to dub, postpunk, and a host of other influences. Some, like Minor Threat, disbanded under the pressure of increasing popularity rather than compromise their music and ideals.

Upon its release in 1985, all of this recent history was brought to bear on the *Salad Days* 7″. But in the lyrics to the title track MacKaye was quick to reject any hint of nostalgia: *On to greener pastures / The core has gotten soft.* It is this refusal to romanticize hardcore's early years that marks *Salad Days* as simultaneously an archival document and a provocation to move forward. The back cover of the 7″ captures this sense of possibility with a photograph by Tomas Squip of Nelson and the Dischord House dog, Susie, literally walking over the horizon, the sky a vast field of white above them. In a black strip to the right, the band name, song titles, and credits are expertly typeset in lowercase Gill Sans, with careful variations in font weight and type size used to create balance and hierarchy. As with Squip's photograph, a generous amount of space separates the text and the Dischord logo, giving the entire composition an openness that is a far cry from the formal density of *Flex Your Head* and the early Minor Threat singles.

It is into this openness, both formal and musical, that a subsequent generation of designers, photographers, musicians, and artists would step, building on the productive energies opened up during the early years of hardcore. From the slab serif fonts of "youth crew" straight edge bands and the neo-tribal graphics of political punk, to the rich 'zine culture that gave rise to Riot Grrrl, the tools of graphic design would be put to use in the shaping of post-hardcore subcultures that were as diverse visually as they were musically. Indeed, for teenagers like myself—and I suspect there is a new crop every year—the landscape of underground music and culture remained wide-open territory. In particular, Dischord's releases over the next several years, many of them designed or art directed by Nelson, would conjure an image of the maturing D.C. scene—a quasi-utopian community of musical innovation and activism existing in a kind of perpetual autumn—that would serve as a creative and imaginative touchstone for legions of devoted fans.

In this regard the benefit compilation *State of the Union*, released by Dischord in April 1989, might serve as a provisional summary statement of the scene's development over the course of its first decade, featuring tracks by groundbreaking D.C. bands like

recorded 12·14·83
recorded 12·14·83
at inner ear studios.
engineer · don zientara
mix · jeff, lyle, don
photos · back · tomas
front · glen e. friedman
art · jeff nelson
dischord fifteen

©℗ 1985 Dischord

3819 beecher st. nw, washir

Lyrics by Ian MacKaye 9·83   ©&℗
JIM SAAH
DOUG HUMISKI
CYNTHIA CONNOLLY
CYNTHIA CONNOLLY

Jeff   ©℗ 1982,19
Lyle
Brian
Ian

Dear Mark —

Hi there —

... The only shirts I still have are: EGG HUNT,
MINOR THREAT & DISCHORD. #8.00 each, postpaid.

I learned most of my graphic stuff just by doing
it. I tried to work at a printer's, but they wanted
someone experienced + a union member. I guess
I'd take some graphic arts/design/advertising courses.

Good luck —

JN

184.219 [above]
Postcard from Jeff Nelson
to Mark Owens, July 1988

185.220 [opposite]
Orginal sketch for the **Minor
Threat** *Salad Days* 7", 1985;
Illustration by Jeff Nelson

Three, Shudder to Think, Soulside, Ignition, One Last Wish, and Fugazi. Around this time I graduated from high school and prepared for college with the vague notion that I wanted to study graphic design. On the pretext of inquiring about ordering a T-shirt I wrote to Jeff Nelson asking for any advice he might have. He responded with a polite postcard informing me that shirts were $8 postpaid and that he had learned most of his design skills "just by doing it." "I guess I'd take some graphic arts / design / advertising courses. Good luck," he concluded. Hardly the inspirational words I was looking for. But then again, what more did I expect him to say? As I would come to realize as I started to design record covers for my own small label and, gradually, began to think of myself as a graphic designer, the example of Nelson's work for Dischord, and in particular *Salad Days*, had already given me all the guidance I really needed.

01 The list is a long one. See especially: Steven Blush, *American Hardcore: A Tribal History.* Feral House, 2001.; Marc Spitz and Brendan Mullen, *We Got the Neutron Bomb: The Untold Story of L.A. Punk.* Three Rivers Press, 2001.; Michael Azerrad, *This Band Could Be Your Life.* Back Bay Books, 2002.; Brendan Mullen, ed. *Lexicon Devil: The Fast Times and Short Life of Darby Crash and the Germs.* Feral House, 2002.; Peter Saville, *Designed by Peter Saville.* Princeton Architectural Press, 2003.; Mark Andersen and Mark Jenkins, *Dance of Days: Two Decades of Punk in the Nation's Capital.* Akashic Books, 2003.; Andy Greenwald, *Nothing Feels Good: Punk Rock, Teenagers, and Emo.* St. Martin's Griffin, 2003.; Tim Irwin, *We Jam Econo: The Story of the Minutemen.* 2006.; Simon Reynolds, *Rip It Up and Start Again: Postpunk 1978-1984.* Penguin Books, 2006.; Rob Young, *Rough Trade: Labels Unlimited.* Black Dog Publishing, 2006.; Nadine Monem, *Riot Grrrl: Revolution Girl Style Now!* Black Dog, 2007.
02 Interview with Jeff Nelson, November 2007.
03 Mark Owens, "Graphics Incognito." *Dot Dot Dot* #12, Summer 2006. p. 45-54.
04 Interview with Jeff Nelson, November 2007.
05 In the light of the recent nationally-distributed documentary *American Hardcore* [Paul Rachman, 2006], which in its comprehensive reach tends to flatten out the differences between bands and scenes, it is important to remember that even early on hardcore was characterized by a surprising level of variety. Groups like Austin, Texas band The Big Boys, who played funk-punk and hardcore fronted by an openly gay lead singer—to name just one—are a case in point.

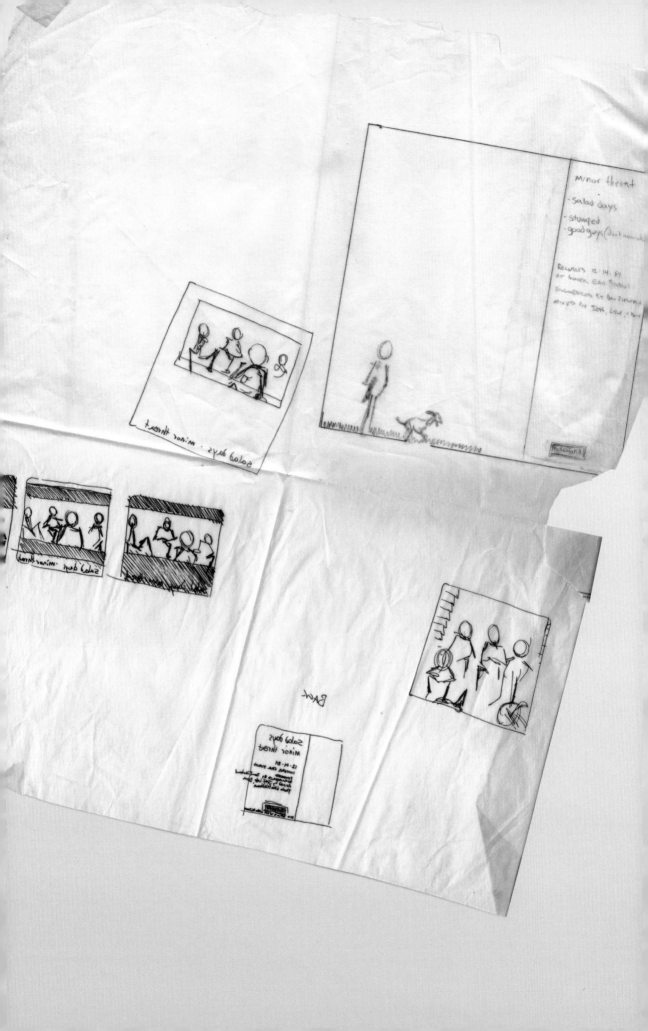

So serious about the stuff we lack /
Dwell upon our memories but there are no facts.

Minor Threat "Salad Days"

188.221
Agnostic Front *Live At CBGB* 12", In-Effect Records, 1989

188.222
Born Against *Nine Patriotic Hymns For Children* 12",
Vermiform Records, 1991

188.223
Warzone *Don't Forget the Struggle, Don't Forget the Streets* 12",
Fist Records, 1987

188.224
Agnostic Front *Liberty & Justice For...* 12",
Combat Core /Relativity Records, 1987

188.225
Hüsker Dü *In a Free Land* 7", New Alliance Records, 1982

188.226
Hüsker Dü *Land Speed Record* 12", New Alliance Records, 1982

188.227
Armed Citizens *Make Sense* 7", Big City/Make Sense Records, 1983

188.228
Infest *s/t* 7", self released, 1988

188.229
Wasted Youth *Reagan's In* 12", ICI / Sanoblast Records, 1981

188.230
Voice of Reason *Parody To the Righteous* 7", Mindseye Records, 1991

188.231
M.I.A. *Murder In A Foreign Place* 12", Alternative Tentacles, 1984

188.232
MDC *Multi-Death Corporations* 7", R Radical Records, 1983

189.233
Charred Remains aka Man is the Bastard/Bleeding Rectum
split 12", self released, 1992

189.234
Cro-Mags *The Age of Quarrel* 12", Profile/Rock Hotel Records, 1986

189.235
Agnostic Front *Victim In Pain* 12", Ratcage Records, 1984

189.236
Econochrist *It Runs Deep* 7", Truant Records, 1988

189.237
Infest *Mankind* 7", Draw Blank Records, 1991

189.238
Crucifix *Dehumanization* 12", Corpus Christi Records, 1983

189.239
Go! *Your Power Means Nothing* 7", King Fish Records, 1990

189.240
Crossed Out *s/t* 7", Slapham Records, 1991

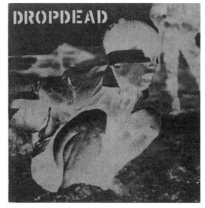

189.241
Dropdead / Crossed Out *Split* 5", Rhetoric/Selfless/
Crust Records, 1993

189.242
Infest *Slave* 12", Deep Six Records, 1988

189.243
God's Chosen People compilation 12", Old Glory Records, 1993

189.244
Flagman *Restraint* 7", Watermark Records, 1993

190.245
Bad Brains *Quickness* 12", Caroline Records, 1989

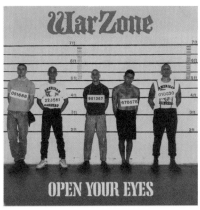

190.246
Warzone *Open Your Eyes* 12", Caroline Records, 1988

190.247
Kraut *An Adjustment To Society* 12", Cabbage Records, 1982

190.248
Iceburn *Burn / Fall* 7", Victory Records, 1991

190.249
Sheer Terror *Just Can't Hate Enough* 12", Blackout! Records, 1990

190.250
Supertouch *The Earth Is Flat* 12", Revelation Records, 1990

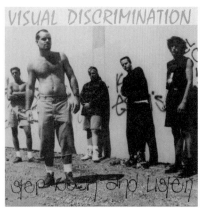

190.251
Visual Discrimination *Step Back And Listen* 12", Nemisis Records, 1988

190.252
Sick of It All *s/t* 7", Revelation Records, 1987

190.253
Suicidal Tendencies *s/t* 12", Frontier Records, 1983

190.254
Sub Society *Relaxin'* 7", Vinyl Communications, 1991

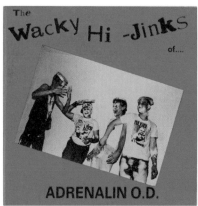

190.255
Adrenalin O.D. *Wacky Hi-Jinks Of....* 12", Buy Our Records, 1984

190.256
Meatmen *Rock 'N' Roll Juggernaut* 12", Caroline Records, 1986

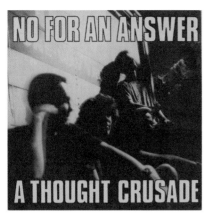

191.257
No For An Answer *A Thought Crusade* 12", Hawker/
Roadrunner Records, 1988

191.258
Agent Orange *Living In Darkness* 12", Posh Boy Records, 1981

191.259
Samhain *Initium* 12", Plan 9 Records, 1984

191.260
Swiz *Hell Yes I Cheated* 12", Sammich Records, 1989

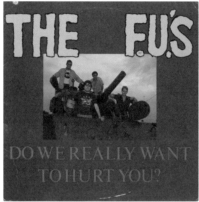

191.261
F.U.s *Do We Really Want To Hurt You* 12", Gasatanka/
Enigma, Records, 1984

191.262
JFA *Live 1984 Tour* 12", Placebo Records, 1984

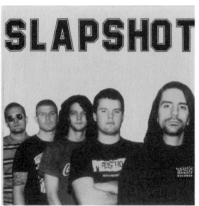

191.263
Slapshot *Firewalker* 7", Taang! Records, 1990

191.264
Scream *This Side Up* 12", Sixth International Records/
Dischord Records, 1985

191.265
Go!/Bad Trip split 7", Skene! Records, 1990

191.266
Youth of Today *We're Not in This Alone* 12", Caroline Records, 1988

191.267
Gang Green *P.M.R.C. SUCKS* 12", HIM Records, 1985

191.268
Madball *Droppin' Many Suckers* 7", Wreckage Records, 1993

192.269
New York Hardcore: Where The Wild Things Are compilation 12",
Blackout Records, 1989

192.270
Chain of Strength *What Holds Us Apart* 7",
First Strike Records, 1991

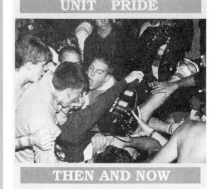

192.271
Unit Pride *Then And Now* 7", Point Blank Records, 1990

192.272
Youth of Today *Break Down the Walls* 12",
Wishingwell Records, 1986

192.273
Agnostic Front *United Blood* 7", self released, 1983

192.274
Iron Cross *Skinhead Glory* 7", Skin Flint Records, 1982

192.275
Inside Out *No Spiritual Surrender* 7", Revelation Records, 1990

192.276
Burn *s/t* 7", Revelation Records, 1990

192.277
Powerhouse *s/t* 7", New Age Records, 1989

192.278
Brotherhood *No Tolerance For Ignorance* 7", Skate Edge Records, 1988

192.279
Double-O *s/t* 7", R&B/Dischord Records, 1983

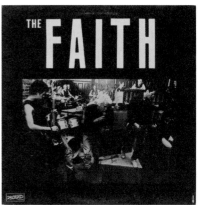

192.280
Faith / Void *split* 12", Dischord Records, 1983

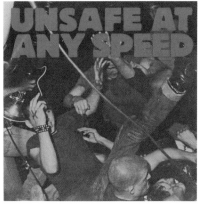

193.281
Unsafe At Any Speed compilation 7", Modern Method Records, 1982

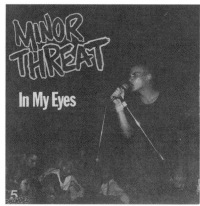

193.282
Minor Threat *In My Eyes* 7", Dischord Records, 1981

193.283
Faith *Subject To Change* 12", Dischord Records, 1983

193.284
7 Seconds *The Crew* 12", Better Youth Organization Records, 1984

193.285
Soulside *Trigger* 12", Dischord Records, 1988

193.286
Government Issue *Make An Effort* 7",
Fountain of Youth Records, 1983

193.287
T.S.O.L. *s/t* 12", Posh Boy Records, 1981

193.288
Youth of Today *Can't Close My Eyes* 7", Positive Force Records, 1985

193.289
Voice of Thousands compilation 12", Conversion Records, 1990

193.290
Turning Point *It's Always Darkest....* 12", New Age Records, 1990

193.291
State of Alert *No Policy* 7", Dischord Records, 1981

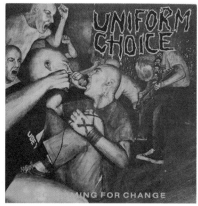

193.292
Uniform Choice *Screaming For Change* 12",
Wishingwell Records, 1986

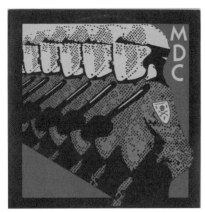

194.293
MDC *Millions of Dead Cops* 12", R Radical Records, 1982

194.294
Verbal Assault *Tiny Giants* 7", Giant Records, 1988

194.295
Econochrist *Another Victim* 7", Vermiform Records, 1991

194.296
Side by Side *You're Only Young Once* 7", Revelation Records, 1988

194.297
Dag Nasty *Wig Out At Denkos* 12", Dischord Records, 1987

194.298
Articles of Faith *Give Thanks* 12", Reflex Records, 1984

194.299
Verbal Assault *Trial* 12", Konkurrel Records, 1987

194.300
Ignition *Sinker /Anger Means* 12", Southern Records, 1988

194.301
Soulside *Bass* 7", Dischord Records, 1989

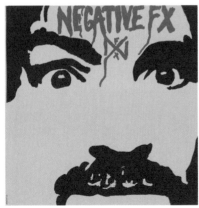

194.302
Negative FX *s/t* 12", Taang! Records, 1984

194.303
Slapshot *Same Mistake* 7", Taang! Records, 1988

194.304
Swiz *s/t* 12", Sammich Records, 1988

195.305
JFA *Blatant Localism* 7", Placebo Records, 1981

195.306
Code of Honor *What Are We Gonna Do?* 7", Subterranean Records, 1982

195.307
Agression *Don't Be Mistaken* 12", Better Youth Organization Records, 1983

195.308
Gang Green *Skate To Hell/Alcohol* 7", Taang Records, 1985

195.309
Doggy Style *Don't Hit Me Up* 12", Triple X Records, 1988

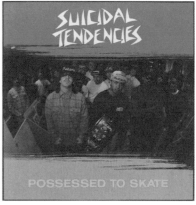

195.310
Suicidal Tendencies *Possessed To Skate* 12", Caroline Records, 1987

195.311
Release / Courage split 7", Threshold Records, 1990

195.312
Breakdown *The '87 Demo* 7", Noiseville / Blackout Records, 1990

195.313
Underdog *Demos* 12", Far Out Records, 1991

195.314
Faction *Yesterday Is Gone* 7", IM Records, 1983

195.315
Faction *Epitaph* 12", Mystic Thrash Records, 1986

195.316
Skate Rock Vol. 4: Smash compilation 12", *Thrasher/* High Speed Productions, 1986

196.317
Effigies *Remains Nonviewable* 7", Ruthless Records, 1982

196.318
D.I. *Horse Bites Dog Cries* 12", Triple X Records, 1985

196.319
Excel *Split Image* 12", Suicidal Records, 1987

196.320
Uniform Choice *Region of Ice* 7", Giant Records, 1988

196.321
Infest *Slave* 12", Off The Disk Records, 1988

196.322
Leeway *Born To Expire* 12", Profile Records, 1988

196.323
SSD *How We Rock* 12", Modern Method Records, 1984

196.324
Killing Time *Brightside* 12", In-Effect/Relativity Records, 1989

196.325
Suicidal Tendencies *Join The Army* 12", Caroline Records, 1987

196.326
Rich Kids On L.S.D. *Revenge Is A Beautiful Feeling* 12",
Destiny Records, 1989

196.327
Shelter *Perfection Of Desire* 12", Revelation Records, 1990

196.328
Attitude Adjustment *American Paranoia* 12",
Pusmort Records, 1986

197.329
No Mercy *Bloodshed Love Runs Red* 12", Suicidal Records, 1987

197.330
Cleanse The Bacteria compilation 12", Pusmort Records, 1985

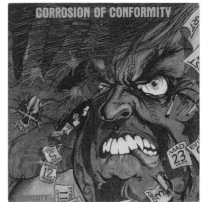

197.331
Corrosion of Conformity *Animosity* 12", Metal Blade Records, 1986

197.332
Septic Death *Need So Much Attention* 12", Pusmort Records, 1984

197.333
Econochrist *Ruination* 12", Very Small Records, 1990

197.334
Necros *Conquest for Death* 7", Touch and Go Records, 1983

197.335
Batallion of Saints *Fighting Boys* 12", Nutrons Records, 1982

197.336
Batallion of Saints *Second Coming* 12", Nutrons Records/
Enigma Records, 1984

197.337
Misfits *Earth A.D / Wolfsblood* 12", Plan 9 Records, 1983

197.338
Christ on Parade *Sounds of Nature* 12", Pusmort Records, 1985

197.339
Empty Skulls Vol. 2: The Wound Deepens compilation 12",
Fartblossom Enterprises Records, 1986

197.340
Dirty Rotten Imbeciles *Violent Pacification* 7", Dirty Rotten
Records, 1984

198.341
Payback *Draw The Line* 7", Outer Limit Productions Records, 1989

198.342
Grudge *Project-Ex* 7", Jism Records, 1989

198.343
In Your Face *The Grub* 7", Common Cause Records, 1989

198.344
Crucial Youth *Straight and Loud* 7", Faith Records, 1987

198.345
Token Entry *Ready or Not Here We Come* 7", self released, 1985

198.346
Nardcore compilation 12", Mystic Records, 1984

198.347
Justice League *Think Or Sink* 7",
Fartblossom Enterprises Records, 1985

198.348
No Control at the Country Club Live compilation 7",
Nemisis Records, 1990

198.349
Underdog *s/t* 7", New Beginning Records, 1986

198.350
SS Decontrol *Get It Away* 12", XClaim Records, 1983

198.351
D.R.I. *Dealing With It* 12", Death/Metal Blade
Restless Records, 1985

198.352
7 Seconds *Committed For Life* 7", Squirtdown Records, 1983

199.353
The Mob *Upset the System* 7", Mob Style Records, 1982

199.354
Meatmen *We're The Meatmen... And You Suck!* 12",
Touch and Go Records, 1982

199.355
Crucial Youth *Crucial Yule* 12", Faith Records, 1988

199.356
The Mob *Step Forward* 7", Mob Style Records, 1983

199.357
7 Seconds *Walk Together, Rock Together* 12",
Positive Force Records, 1985

199.358
Crucial Youth *The Posi-Machine* 12", New Red Archives, 1988

199.359
Murphy's Law *Back With A Bong* 12", Profile Records, 1989

199.360
Connecticut Fun compilation 12", Incas Records, 1985

199.361
Token Entry *From Beneath the Streets* 12",
Positive Force Records, 1987

199.362
Pagan Babies *Next* 12", Hawker Records, 1988

199.363
X Marks the Spot compilation 7", Smorgasbord Records, 1988

199.364
Battered Citizens *Rolling With the Punches* 7",
Overkill Records, 1989

200.365
Toxic Reasons *Independence* 12", Risky Records, 1982

200.366
Citizens Arrest *Colossus* 12", Wardance Records, 1991

200.367
Only The Strong compilation 12", Victory Records, 1990

200.368
Life's Blood *Defiance* 12", Combined Effort Records, 1988

200.369
Murders compilation 7",Vermiform Records, 1990

200.370
Look At All the Children Now... compilation 12",
Evacuate Records, 1990

200.371
Rat Music for Rat People Vol. 2 compilation 12",
CD Presents Records, 1984

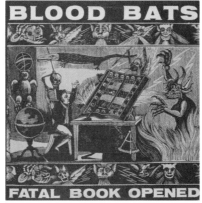

200.372
Blood Bats *Fatal Book Opened* 12", Hellfire Records, 1987

200.373
Integrity *Those Who Fear Tomorrow* 12", Overkill Records, 1991

200.374
Shades Apart *s/t* 12", Wishingwell Records, 1988

200.375
Worlds Collide *Object Of Desire* 7", Victory Records, 1992

200.376
Reason to Believe *When Reason Sleeps Demons Dance* 12",
Nemesis Records, 1990

201.377
Gray Matter *Food For Thought* 12", R&B Records, 1985

201.378
Scream *Still Screaming* 12", Dischord Records, 1982

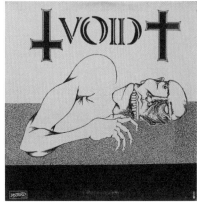

201.379
Void/Faith split 12", Dischord Records, 1982

201.380
Living on the Edge compilation 7", Positive Vibes Records, 1990

201.381
Mindwar/Evolve split 7", Round Two Records, 1992

201.382
Sticks and Stones/Life's Blood split 7", Radcore/ Forefront Records, 1990

201.383
Gray Matter *s/t* double 7", Dischord /WGNS Records, 1990

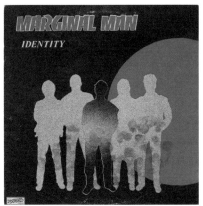

201.384
Marginal Man *Identity* 12", Dischord Records, 1984

201.385
Merel *s/t* 12", Gern Blandsten, 1992

201.386
End to End *s/t* 7", Foundation Records, 1990

201.387
Voice of Reason *Gear* 7", Selfless Records, 1992

201.388
Bad Trip *Positively Bad* 7", Bell Bottom Records, 1989

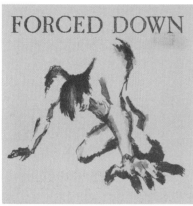

202.389
Forced Down *Rise* 7", Down Side/
Vinyl Communications Records, 1990

202.390
Articles of Faith *In This Life* 12", Lone Wolf Records, 1987

202.391
Lifetime *s/t* 7", New Age Records, 1991

202.392
Drift Again *s/t* 12", Network Sound Records, 1991

202.393
Kingpin *Holding Tomorrow* 7", Suburban Voice Records, 1991

202.394
Shadow Season *s/t* 7", Harvest Records, 1992

202.395
Reptile House *Listen To the Powersoul* 12", Merkin Records, 1989

202.396
Die Kreuzen *s/t* 12", Touch and Go Records, 1984

202.397
No Escape/Turning Point split 7", Temperance Records, 1991

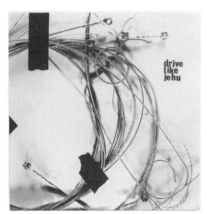

202.398
Drive Like Jehu *Bullet Train To Vegas* 7", Merge Records, 1992

202.399
Second Story Window *s/t* 7", Gravity Records, 1993

202.400
7 Seconds *Praise* 12", Positive Force Records, 1987

203.401
Fear of Smell compilation 12", Vermiform Records, 1993

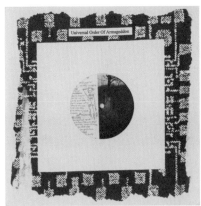

203.402
Universal Order of Armageddon *s/t* 12", Gravity Records, 1994

203.403
Angel Hair *s/t* 7", Gravity Records, 1994

203.404
Antioch Arrow *The Lady Is A Cat* 12", Gravity Records, 1993

203.405
Antioch Arrow *In Love With Jets* 12", Gravity Records, 1994

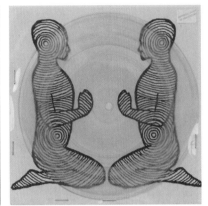

203.406
Universal Order of Armageddon *City* 7",
Vermin Scum Records, 1993

203.407
Mohinder/Nitwits split 7", Unleaded Records, 1994

203.408
Moss Icon *Memorial* 7", Vermin Scum Records, 1991

203.409
Heroin *s/t* 7", Gravity Records, 1992

203.410
John Henry West *s/t* 7", Gravity Records, 1993

203.411
Heroin *All About Heroin* 7", Down Side /
Vinyl Communications Records, 1991

203.412
Born Against/Universal Order of Armageddon split 7",
Gravity Records, 1993

204.413
Urban Waste *s/t* 7", Mob Style Records, 1982

204.414
Eye for an Eye *Omega Drone* 7", Blackout Records, 1991

204.415
Kingface *Everywhere You Look* 12", Konkurrel Records, 1989

204.416
C.I.A. *God, Guts, Guns* 7", Shmegma Records, 1983

204.417
Bold *s/t* 7"; Revelation Records, 1989

204.418
Verbal Assault *On* 12", Konkurrel Records, 1989

204.419
Major Conflict *s/t* 7", Silent Scream Records, 1993

204.420
108 *Holy Name* 12", Equal Vision Records, 1992

204.421
Faction *Dark Room* 12", IM Records, 1985

204.422
Agent Orange *When You Least Expect It..* 12", Engima Records, 1984

204.423
Strength In Numbers *s/t* 7", Common Sense Records, 1990

204.424
Life Sentence *s/t* 12", Walkthrufyre Records, 1986

205.425
Insted *We'll Make The Difference* 7", Nemisis Records, 1989

205.426
Fury *Resurrection* 7", THD Records, 1991

205.427
Absolution *s/t* 7", Combined Effort Records, 1989

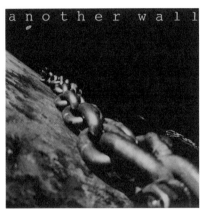

205.428
Another Wall *s/t* 7", Doghouse Records, 1994

205.429
Three *Dark Days Coming* 12", Dischord Records, 1989

205.430
Fuel *Take Effect* 7", Lookout Records, 1990

205.431
Unity *Blood Days* 12", Power House Records, 1991

205.432
It's For Life compilation 12", Consequence Records, 1992

205.433
411 *This Isn't Me* 12", Workshed Records, 1991

205.434
Headfirst *The Enemy* 12", Workshed Records, 1991

205.435
Words to Live By compilation 7", New Age Records, 1991

205.436
Strife *My Fire Burns On* 7", New Age Records, 1992

206.437
Supertouch *Arch Type* [back detail] T-shirt, c.1988

206.438
Supertouch [test shirt] T-shirt, c.1988

206.439
Burn test print T-shirt, c.1990

206.440
Inside Out *Logo* T-shirt, c.1990

206.441
No For An Answer *O.C. Straight Edge* [back detail] T-shirt, c.1988

206.442
Token Entry *Positive Force Records* T-shirt, c.1987

206.443
Unofficial **Bold** *Collegiate Type* T-shirt [small run given to Revelation Records for distribution], c.1988

206.444
Outspoken [one off test print] tank-top, c.1991

206.445
Bl'ast *Power of Expression* T-shirt, c.1986

206.446
Bad Religion *Suffer Tour 1988* T-shirt, c.1988

206.447
Uniform Choice *U.C.* [back detail] T-shirt, c.1988

206.448
Raw Deal *Only the Strong Survive* T-shirt, c.1988

207.449
Absolution *Logo* T-shirt, c.1989

207.450
America's Hardcore *Be Yourself* T-shirt, c.1983

207.451
Chain of Strength *What Holds Us Apart* T-shirt, c.1990

207.452
Smorgasboard Records *Straight Edge* T-shirt, c.1988

207.453
New Age Records *Proud To Be* T-shirt, c.1989

207.454
Smorgasbord Records *Straight Edge* T-shirt, c.1987

207.455
Spirit of Youth *Drugs Kill* T-shirt, c.1987

207.456
Brotherhood *Fuck Racism* T-shirt, c.1988

207.457
Step Forward Records *Drug Free Youth* T-shirt, c.1989

207.458
Wide Awake *[front detail]* T-shirt, c.1988

207.459
Justice League *Be Yourself* tank-top, c.1984

207.460
Unit Pride *Holding On Strong* T-shirt, c.1989

208.461
Chain of Strength *What Holds Us Apart* [back detail] T-shirt, c.1990

208.462
Chain of Strength *Has The Edge Gone Dull?*
[back detail] T-shirt, c.1990

208.463
Gorilla Biscuits *Banana Core* [back detail] T-shirt, c.1988

208.464
Dischord Records *Dischord Ad* T-shirt, c.1986

208.465
Judge *Bringin' It Down* [back detail] T-shirt, c.1989

208.466
Mouthpiece *Straight Edge* T-shirt, c.1992

208.467
Turning Point *Hi-Impact Records* [back detail] T-shirt, c.1988

208.468
Strife *New Age Records* T-shirt, c.1992

208.469
Youth of Today *Break Down the Walls* [back detail] T-shirt, c.1987

208.470
Uniform Choice *Screaming For Change* T-shirt, c.1986

208.471
Youth of Today *Break Down the Walls Summer Tour 1987*
T-shirt, c.1987

208.472
Wide Awake [back detail] T-shirt, c.1988

209.473
Triggerman [back detail] T-shirt, c.1991

209.474
411 *Say It* T-shirt, c.1991

209.475
Carry Nation *Face The Nation* T-shirt, c.1989

209.476
Headfirst *The Enemy* T-shirt, c.1991

209.477
No For An Answer *I Spy* T-shirt, c.1989

209.478
Addiction [front detail] T-shirt, c.1989

209.479
Econochrist *Government Has Blood on Its Hands*
[back detail] T-shirt, c.1991

209.480
Wrecking Crew *Wolf* [front detail] T-shirt, c.1988

209.481
7 Seconds *Ourselves Tour 1988* T-shirt, c.1988

209.482
Struggle *Politicians Are In Season* [back detail] T-shirt, c.1992

209.483
Beyond *No Longer At Ease* [back detail] T-shirt, c.1988

209.484
Swiz *Script Logo* T-shirt, c.1989

210.485
Doggy Style [back detail] T-shirt, c.1985

210.486
Breakdown *Causin' More Trouble In '88* T-shirt, c.1988

210.487
Bold *Join The Fight* T-shirt, c.1987

210.488
Crucial Youth *Skatin' With Satan* [back detail] T-shirt, c.1987

210.489
Gorilla Biscuits *Banana Core* tank-top, c.1988

210.490
Circle Jerks *World Tour 1987* T-shirt, c.1987

210.491
MDC *Tour Amerikka 1988* [front detail] T-shirt, c.1988

210.492
Pressure Release [back detail] T-shirt, c.1987

210.493
Release *The Pain Inside* T-shirt, c.1989

210.494
Meatmen *Huge Cock* T-shirt, c.1983

210.495
Pillsbury Hardcore *Cup 'O' Java* T-shirt, c.1985

210.496
Big Boys *Skatin'* T-shirt, c.1982

211.497
Justice League *Obsession Kills* T-shirt, c.1985

211.498
Grim *Face of Betrayal Tour 1989* T-shirt, c.1989

211.499
Uniform Choice *Straight and Alert* T-shirt, c.1986

211.500
Underdog *Underdog NYC* T-shirt, c.1988

211.501
Wide Awake *Hold True* T-shirt, c.1988

211.502
Bad Brains *Quickness Tour 1989* T-shirt, c.1989

211.503
MDC *Tour Amerikka 1988* [back detail] T-shirt, c.1988

211.504
JFA *Skate Tour '85* T-shirt, c.1985

211.505
Insight *Standing Strong* T-shirt, c.1989

211.506
Unit Pride *Tour 1989* [back detail] T-shirt, c.1989

211.507
Crucial Youth *Crucial Youth Skate Crew* [back detail] T-shirt, c.1988

211.508
Insted *Bonds of Friendship* T-shirt, c.1987

212.509
Rites of Spring *Rose* T-shirt, c.1986

212.510
Reason to Believe *The Next Door* T-shirt, c.1988

212.511
Universal Order of Armageddon T-shirt, c.1992

212.512
Sticks and Stones T-shirt, c.1991

212.513
Universal Order of Armageddon T-shirt, c.1993

212.514
Ebullition Records *Logo* [back detail] T-shirt, c.1992

212.515
Quicksand *Melinda Beck woodcut* T-shirt, c.1992

212.516
Uniform Choice *Staring at the Sun* [back detail] T-shirt, c.1988

212.517
Dag Nasty *Field Day Tour 1988* T-shirt, c.1988

212.518
Freewill [back detail] T-shirt, c.1988

212.519
Unity *You Are One* [back detail] T-shirt, c.1986

212.520
3 [test shirt] T-shirt, c.1987

213.521
Los Crudos *¡Ni Olvido Ni Perdon!* [back detail] T-shirt, c.1993

213.522
Burn *Shall Be Judged* T-shirt, c.1990

213.523
Burn *Burning Car* tank-top, c.1990

213.524
Bad Brains *RIOR Cassette Cover* tank-top, c.1985

213.525
Uniform Choice *A Wish To Dream* T-shirt, c.1987

213.526
Hard Stance *Face Reality* T-shirt, c.1989

213.527
Scream *Banging the Drum Fall 1987* t-shirt, 1987

213.528
Youth Brigade *Sound and Fury Tour 1983* t-shirt, 1983

213.529
Corrossion of Conformity *Logo* t-shirt, 1987

213.530
Cro-Mags *The Age of Quarrel* T-shirt, c.1987

213.531
American Standard *New Jersey* T-shirt, c.1988

213.532
End to End T-shirt, c.1989

Contributors

Matt Anderson
Heroin, Gravity Records
In 1991 Matt founded Gravity Records as a vehicle to release several of the budding bands in San Diego, California including his own band, Heroin. Gravity's early releases grew to define a new sound in hardcore rooted in tradition but boasting a chaotic sound that showcased a new approach to hardcore. And they looked noticeably different with hand screen-printed covers and unique packaging. Matt recently played in Spacehorse and lives in San Diego where he continues to run Gravity Records.
gravityrec.com

Al Barkley
Industrial Cows, Contrast,
Brave New World, X (fanzine)
As an isolated skateboarder in Rhode Island, Al started *Shredder* skate 'zine with a friend in 1986 and was instantly hooked. That obsession lead to his own label and distro which eventually grew into Contrast Records, a punk/hardcore record store in Providence, Rhode Island. After the Contrast store closed in 2004, Al shifted focus and began traveling the world.
albarkley.com

Brett Beach
Hardware **fanzine**
Brett co-founded *Hardware* fanzine with David Koenig and ran In My Blood Records which released the *Division One Champs* 7" by Floorpunch. He currently lives in Red Bank, New Jersey.

David Bett
David began designing for the independent music industry in his role as art director for Relativity Records in 1987. He then worked on a string of recognizable releases for Revelation Records and In-Effect Records including Youth of Today, Bold, Judge, and Sick of It All. He is now a Grammy-nominated director of design at Columbia Records/Sony BMG working with Bruce Springsteen, Patti Smith, Aerosmith, and AC/DC, as well as emerging artists. Dave is currently a married father of three living in Long Island, New York.

Brian Brannon
JFA
In 1981, at the tender age of 14, Brian Brannon snuck out of his bedroom window to check out a punk show at the Hate House in Phoenix, Arizona. More than 27 years

later, Brian continues to sing for forefathers of the skate punk movement, JFA. Brian has worked as staff writer, art director and music editor of *Thrasher* magazine, editor for *Evidence* magazine, skateboarding editor for Bluetorch TV, editor of the *Seal Beach Sun* newspaper, marketing manager for The Firm Skateboards, and production manager for Birdhouse Skateboards, where he produced the 2007 skate video The Beginning. He is now living in Huntington Beach, California, with his wife, daughter, and two Rottweilers. Brian skates and surfs every chance he gets and continues to freelance for *The Skateboard Mag*, *Concrete Wave*, and Michael Cornelius' website skaterock.com.

Chris Bratton
Justice League, Chain of Strength,
No For An Answer, Inside Out,
Drive Like Jehu, Statue
Chris Bratton has founded and played drums for several influential California hardcore bands including Chain of Strength and Inside Out. Chris joined former members of Scream in the band Wool in the early 1990s. Chris is currently living in Los Angeles, California where he jams regularly with London May of Samhain.

Shawn Brown
Dag Nasty, Swiz, Fury
Upon leaving Dag Nasty's original line up in 1986 Shawn formed Swiz with some Washington, D.C. locals, including a guitarist named Jason Farrell whom he recognized from a local skateboard shop. After several releases and tours, Swiz disbanded in the early 1990s. The members reformed under the name Sweetbelly Freakdown in 1996. Shawn also fronted Northern Mistep and Jesuseater. He is currently a full-time tattoo artist at Great Southern Tattoos in College Park, Maryland.

Erik Brunetti
Erik is an American artist and designer, best known for his foundation of the brand FUCT. He is credited as a creator of subversive streetwear, a style of designing stemming from the situationist movement which involves subtly changing or re-appropriating various pop culture themes and icons, as well as anti-government, anti-religion campaigns. Growing up in Philadelphia, Brunetti played in various punk bands. In 1984 while still attending high school he discovered graffiti and started bombing. He has written the tag DEN ONE for over 20 years.

Tom Capone
Beyond, Bold, Shelter, Quicksand
Tom Capone grew up in Long Island, New York where he founded the band Beyond at age 16. He played in several hardcore bands before forming Quicksand with Walter Schreifels, one of the first post-hardcore bands to sign to a major label. After touring the world and recording a 7" and two major label albums with Quicksand he went on to join Handsome which featured members of Helmet and Cro-Mags. In 2002 Tom joined the band Instruction. He is now living in upstate New York and getting ready to unleash a promising new band.

Christopher Cannon
Christopher is a graphic designer living in Brooklyn, New York with his wife and baby boy. He works on a wide variety of projects and freelances on the side as Isotope 221.

Chris Casali
Co-founder of How's Your Edge and The Collection Space. Chris is married and a proud father living in Rhode Island.
howsyouredge.com
thecollectionspace.com

Curtis Casella
Taang! Records
After buying Chris Spedding and the Vibrators' "Pogo Dancing" b/w "The Pose" 45 in 1976, Curtis abandoned glam and dove straight into punk rock. He founded Taang! Records in 1984 releasing Gang Green's debut 7" *Sold Out*. He eventually opened a Taang! store front in Harvard Square in Cambridge, Massachusetts. The store relocated to San Diego, California in the early 1990s where Curtis lives and continues to operate the label and store.
taang.com

Jordan Cooper
Revelation Records
Jordan Cooper, started Revelation Records with Ray Cappo in 1987 to release Warzone's debut 7". The label relocated from New Haven, Connecticut to Huntington Beach, California in the early 1990s where Jordan continues to run the day-to-day operations.
revelationrecords.com

Chase E. Corum
Chase lives in Newport Beach, California where he is an attorney, a boat captain, and the owner of Prime Directive Records.
myspace.com/primedirectiverecords

Sean Cronan

Sean grew up in Connecticut skateboarding and photographing bands like Endpoint, Split Lip, By the Grace of God, Falling Forward, Another Wall, Lifetime, Texas is the Reason, Supertouch, Mouthpiece, and Ressurection. He has previously worked as a staff photographer for Tum Yeto Inc., *Transworld Skateboarding*, and *Big Brother*. Currently, Sean is the staff photographer for Zoo York skateboards.
seancronanphotography.com

Vic DiCara
Beyond, Inside Out, Shelter, 108, *The Enquirer* fanzine

Vic DiCara currently plays in the reformed 108. Previously he has worked in web development and, in early 2008 Vic began a career as a Vedic Astrologer. He lives in Escondido, California with his family.
static-void.com

Mike Down
Amenity, Forced Down, Down Side Records

Raised in San Diego, California, Mike founded Down Side records and the Down Organization, booking hundreds of shows at all ages venues. He has since lived in Los Angeles, Las Vegas and New York, working as a solo artist, producer, promoter, and nightlife specialist. He has recorded with Sean Paul, the Pharcyde, and DJ Rob Dinero.
myspace.com/mikedown

Courtney Dubar

Courtney began screen-printing merchandise for Uniform Choice, and the other bands on his brother Pat's Wishingwell Records label, in a shed in his parent's backyard. He eventually started his own screen-printing company which has blossomed into several successful business ventures. Courtney currently lives in Southern California.

Pat Dubar
Uniform Choice, Unity, Wishingwell Records

In the mid-1980s Pat consulted Ian MacKaye about releasing his band Uniform Choice's debut record on Dischord Records. Dischord's policy for only releasing bands native to Washington, D.C. inspired Pat to start Wishingwell Records, which became the home for several Southern California hardcore bands including Uniform Choice, Unity, and Insted. Pat currently lives in Southern California.

Kevin Egan
Beyond, 1.6 Band, The Last Crime

Kevin has been working in television for the last six years, most notably on the daytime talk show *The View*. He currently lives in Austin, Texas where he spends too much money at the amply stocked record stores the city has to offer. Kevin's current musical project is the acoustic outfit Twenty Four Thousand Dollars.

Jason Farrell
Swiz, Fury, Bluetip

Jason's passion for music, skateboarding, and graphic design started in the early 1980s and led him to a career as an art director, designer, and filmmaker. His signature guitar playing and design work continues to inspire and evolve. Jason currently lives in Los Angeles, California and plays guitar in Retisonic.
retisonic.com
jasonfarrelldesign.com

Jon Field
Up Front, Grip, Dayspring, Cycle

Jon currently resides in Richmond, Virginia with his wife and two daughters where he works as a web designer.

Joe D. Foster
Unity, Ignite

After playing guitar for Orange County, California hardcore band Unity in the mid 1980s, Joe began a successful modeling career. In the early 1990s his renewed interest in playing traditional Orange County hardcore he grew up on led him to form Ignite. He currently lives in Southern California.

Glen E. Friedman

Since 1976 Glen has captured some of the most iconic moments in punk, hardcore, skateboarding and hip-hop. He is internationally known for his photographs of Fugazi, Black Flag, Ice-T, Minor Threat, Bad Brains, Beastie Boys, Run-DMC, and Public Enemy, as well as old school skateboarders Tony Alva, Jay Adams, Alan "Ollie" Gelfand, Duane Peters, and Stacy Peralta. Not only was he in the right places at an extraordinary number of appropriate times, he has helped define the moment and movements he was caught up in. His process was much more incendiary than it was documentary. Glen has published several books of his photography with his company Burning Flags Press, most recently *Keep Your Eyes Open*, a compilation of his photographs of Fugazi.
burningflags.com

Mike Gitter
***xXx* fanzine**

Mike's history has been a 25 year straight line from self-publishing *xXx* fanzine in his native Boston suburbs in the early 1980s through overseeing the careers of several bands including Opeth, Megadeth and Killswitch Engage. After working as a rock journalist for everyone from *Thrasher* to *Rolling Stone* he relocated to New York City where he was recruited by Atlantic Records and began what is still a long-running and successful career as an A&R man. These days he's married, has four cats and is living in New Jersey.
myspace.com/thegitter

JJ Gonson

JJ started taking photographs of bands in Boston in the mid-1980s. After leaving Boston in 1991 JJ continued to pursue photography but never again specifically of bands for publication purposes. JJ recently returned to her hometown of Cambridge, Massachusetts with her husband and two children where she runs a catering business. Her photos have appeared in *xXx, the Noise, Suburban Voice, Rip, Creem, Thrasher, Rolling Stone*, and *Spin*.

Mel Gooch

Mel was introduced to hardcore in the summer of 1987 while attending summer camp with several members of Pressure Release. She grew up going to the Anthrax and spent many years driving around the East Coast attending countless shows. Mel currently works as a librarian in Brooklyn, New York.

Guav
***Conviction* fanzine, Conviction Records**

Guav published *Conviction* fanzine and ran Conviction Records which released Earth Crisis' debut 7", *All Out War*. Currently he is the art director of the New York office of Bravado Merchandising, a music merchandising company.
actwondesign.com
guav.com

Luke Hoverman
Another Wall

Luke grew up on Connecticut frequenting the Anthrax club and eventually fronted Another Wall in the early-1990s. Currently he lives in New York City where he works as a photographer.
lukehoverman.com

Contributors

Jimmy Johnson
Forced Exposure **fanzine**
Jimmy was the editor and publisher of *Forced Exposure* fanzine from 1982-1990. Currently he is the owner of Forced Exposure distribution in Malden, Massachusetts. Jimmy saw Black Flag at A7, in case anybody asks.
forcedexposure.com.

Casey Jones
Civil Justice, Just Because, Justice League, No For An Answer, Ignite
Casey has forged a twenty-year career playing drums in several hardcore bands as well as singing for Just Because and Justice League. Casey has been on several world tours but his personal crowning achievement was opening for Scream. He currently lives in California.

Christopher Jones
Verbal Assault
Chris was the vocalist for Rhode Island hardcore band Verbal Assault. Following the bands breakup in 1991 Chris received a History degree from the University of Massachusetts, Amherst. Chris also worked as a tour manager for the rock band Belly. He currently lives in Newport, Rhode Island.
verbalassault.com

Tonie Joy
Moss Icon, The Great Unraveling, Born Against, Universal Order of Armageddon
Tonie Joy founded Moss Icon in Annapolis, Maryland in 1986. Moss Icon's sound and imagery sharply contrasted other hardcore bands of the their time with unique output that shunned reference or tradition. Tonie continues to play music there in the band Convocation Of.

Matt Kattman
Kingpin
Matt grew up in Holliston, Massachusetts where, at the age of 15, he was a founding member of the skate rock band Funny Wagon. He followed that with Kingpin, a band that redefined the sound of Boston hardcore in the early-1990s. During that time Matt also sang briefly for Boston hardcore band Endless. He currently lives in Providence, Rhode Island where he is continuing his education at the Rhode Island School of Design and playing in a new yet-to-be-named music project.

Theresa Kelliher
Theresa Kelliher began photographing bands in Boston, Massachusetts during the mid-1980s where she still lives.

Tim Kerr
Big Boys
Tim Kerr played guitar in Austin, Texas' skate rock band The Big Boys in 1978. Throughout his life, he has never felt comfortable with labels and their restrictions. When someone confines him to one label, they do themselves and Tim a disservice. He is painting more than ever now and plays in an Irish and old time string band with friends in Austin and wherever his travels take him. In Tim's own words, "I'm not dead yet. I am still active and as proud as I am of all that has happened before, I hope I haven't seen the best thing yet."
timkerr.net

Richard Labbate
Insted
Rich was part of the Southern California punk scene in the early 1980s. He went on to play bass in the Orange County bands Insted, Lidsville, Crashcart, and Knapsack. Rich is currently doing an old school hardcore project called The Alligators with Steve and Bear of Insted, fronted by Roger Miret of Agnostic Front. He is married and living in Orange County, California where he runs Merch.com, an online store that sells band T-shirts, skateboards, and fashion apparel.
merch.com

Ian MacKaye
The Slinkees, The Teen Idles, Minor Threat, Embrace, Fugazi, Dischord Records
Ian is a co-founder and co-owner of Dischord Records. He continues to work with the label and lives in Washington, D.C. with his partner, Amy Farina. They perform together in The Evens.
dischord.com

Charles Maggio
Rorschach, Gern Blandsten Records
Currently Charles is the lucky husband of Jennifer Klein, and a proud father of twin baby girls Avery and Mira. Charles' straight job is as a Senior Accountant for a wholesale insurance company, but his ancillary passions include selling rare records on eBay, practicing Brazilian Jiu Jitsu and collecting rare punk and hardcore records. He operates the New Jersey based Gern Blandsten Records, a label he founded in 1992.
gernblandsten.com

Dave Mandell
Indecision **fanzine, Indecision Records**
Dave started going to shows in Southern California in the mid-1980s but it was his love of photography that led him to create the *Indecision* fanzine in the early 1990s. Several issues later Dave expanded *Indecision* with the release of Strife's debut 7". Dave lives in Orange County, California but he is consistently traveling as a documentary photographer covering the Ultimate Fighting Championships.
indecisionrecords.com

Robert Mars
Crucial Youth
Also know as "Ollie Grind," Robert played guitar for New Jersey based Crucial Youth, the most successful straight edge parody band to date. As a designer Robert recently created a collection of mens and womens apparel for Lewsader, under the special label "Robert Mars: Hi-Caliber". He has designed for Adidas, Akademiks, PRPS, Ride Snowboards, 5 Boro Skateboards, Bonfire Snowboard Clothing, Element Skateboards, ESPN X Games Division, and numerous other action sports companies. As a painter he has shown in galleries in Tokyo, Munich, Portland, New York, Vancouver, Melbourne, Los Angeles and Austin.
robertmars.com
lewsadercollective.com

Steve Martin
F.U.'s, Straw Dogs, Agnostic Front
Steve started playing in hardcore bands as a teenager in the early-1980s. Steve eventually joined Agnostic Front at the age of 20. He founded the independent public relations firm Nasty Little Man out of his East Village bedroom in 1993. Steve has amassed a roster including Beastie Boys, Foo Fighters and John Joseph of the Cro-Mags. He has also worked with Radiohead, Nine Inch Nails, Beck, the Arcade Fire, Spoon, and Ryan Adams, among others. Steve lives in New York City with his wife Grace, whom he first met at a CBGB matinee "back in the day," as the kids say.

Vique Martin
Simba **fanzine, Simba Records**
Vique Martin is currently living in California and working as the distribution manager at Revelation Records. She wrote *Simba* fanzine and operated Simba Records in the early 1990s to showcase the bands she loved.

Glenn Maryansky
Another Wall
Glenn is a graphic designer and drummer living in Brooklyn, New York. He currently plays drums in the band Blacklist.
listofblack.com

John Mastropaolo
No For An Answer, Unity, Uniform Choice
John's bass playing in No For An Answer, Unity and later Uniform Choice helped forge the sound associated with the late-1980s Orange County straight edge hardcore scene. He is currently living in Long Beach, California.

Tim McMahon
Mouthpiece
Tim lives in Lawrenceville, New Jersey and is the proud parent of two. After the dissolution of Mouthpiece in the mid-1990s he formed a string of bands including Hands Tied and Face the Enemy. Currently Tim sings for Triple Threat, a straight edge hardcore band, operates Livewire Records with bandmate Ed McKirdy, and edits the online fanzine *Double Cross*.
doublecrosswebzine.blogspot.com
livewire-records.com

Chris Minicucci
Chris is a graphic artist from Westfield, Massachusetts. He has played in other influential Boston bands Close Call and Righteous Jams. He currently runs hardcore/punk label Painkiller Records and plays guitar in Mind Eraser.
painkillerrecords.com

Rusty Moore
Rusty is a native of Greensboro, North Carolina. The early-1980s found him immersed in the punk and hardcore movements, where he frequently traveled up and down the East Coast to photograph bands. Rusty often photographed a band's first set, then hiding his camera behind the bar, he would dance for the second set. Rusty is currently a documentary photographer living in Pembroke, Massachusetts.
rustymooreloudfastphoto.com

Michael Murphy
Michael started going to shows in 1984 and still lives and works in Orange County.

Adam Nathanson
Life's Blood, Born Against, Young Pioneers
Adam is a literacy instructor in ESL, GED, and financial literacy, and a graduate student in adult literacy. He is married to Alyssa Murray of Boston with whom he has two daughters, Reina and Bella. Adam plays in Teargas Rock as well as maintaining a blog that espouses his agenda.
stakolee.blogspot.com

Jeff Nelson
The Slinkees, The Teen Idles, Minor Threat, Skewbald/Grand Union, Egg Hunt, Three, Senator Flux, The High-Back Chairs, Dischord Records.
Jeff founded Minor Threat and Dischord Records with Ian MacKaye. He now lives in Toledo, Ohio where he is writing a history of the Q Street Bridge in Washington, D.C. and collecting Jeep memorabilia. After a hiatus from music, Jeff began playing drums again with Fast Piece of Furniture who released their debut record on Adult Swim Records in 2008.
dischord.com
adultswimrecords.com

Joe Nelson
Triggerman, Ignite
Original Orange County California Sloth Crew member, Joe Nelson is working in artist relations for The Merchandise Company in Long Beach, California. He currently fronts The Killing Flame.

Gavin Ogelsby
No For An Answer, Carry Nation, Triggerman, Ignite
Gavin's first illustration commission was for the cover of MIA's *Murder in a Foreign Place* 12" [see 188.231]. He continues to work as an illustrator in Orange County, California and plays guitar in the Killing Flame.

Dan O'Mahony
No For An Answer,
Carry Nation, VoiceBox, 411
Along with fronting several bands including No For An Answer and 411, Dan has written for the *S.I.C. Press* fanzine, *Maximumrocknroll*, published the books *Three Legged Race* and *Four Letter Word* and ran the Workshed Records label.

Tim Owen
Axtion Packed Records, Jade Tree Records
Tim Owen co-founded Jade Tree Records with Darren Walters which he still operates in Wilmington, Delaware.
jadetree.com

Mark Owens
Mark is a designer, writer and filmmaker working between Los Angeles and New York. He grew up in Texas skateboarding and listening to hardcore and ran a small indie label throughout the second half of the 1990s alongside his twin brother, Matt. Mark pursued a PhD in English from Duke University (ABD 1998) before earning his MFA in graphic design from Yale University

in 2000. Mark's essays have appeared in the pages of *Visible Language, Grafik* magazine, and the postpunk/marxist design journal *Dot Dot Dot.* In 2007 he co-edited the catalogue to the exhibition Forms of Inquiry at the Architectural Association in London with Zak Kyes. He has taught at Yale University and Art Center College of Design and is currently an adjunct faculty member at California Institute of the Arts.
lifeofthemind.net

BJ Papas
While attending the Fashion Institute of Technology in Chelsea, BJ used what she had learned in her photography classes to document the underground punk/hardcore scene in New York City. BJ relocated to California where she works as a commercial photographer. Her photographs can be seen in *Rolling Stone, Spin, Guitar World, Blender,* and *Revolver.*
bjpapas.com

Ernie Parada
Token Entry, Black Train Jack
Inspired by Uncle Al of Murphy's Law and Sean Taggart's artwork, Ernie created a unique cartoon-based illustration style that appeared on several album covers in the late 1980s. Ernie lives in Astoria, New York with his wife Sabrina, and son Ernie Jr. By day, Ernie works as an art director and illustrator, and by night he plays in the Arsons.
thearsons.com

Gus Peña
Discipline, Ocean of Mercy
Gus Peña was born in 1969 in Queens, New York. Once upon a time he sang for Discipline and Ocean of Mercy. In the mid-1980s he would most likely be found stage diving on your head. Currently, Gus lives in North Hollywood, California and runs *Chord* magazine among various other endeavors.
chordmagazine.com

Philin Phlash
"Legendary in some circles, yet a virtual unknown to the larger public…" is just one of the "Phacts" you should know. Phlash grew up shooting photographs of his brother Springa's band SSD. He went on to document live music, night life, and celebrities in his trademark "in your face style." Phlash "was in the pit dodging bodies and battling bouncers" to get the shot. He has been published in Spin, the *Chicago Tribune,* the *Chicago Sun-Times,* and *The Boston Globe.*
philinphlash.com

Contributors

Daniel Assan Piwowarczyk
Daniel is a New York-based graphic designer and (pretentious asshole) record collector. Growing up in São Paulo, Brazil he played in the band Newspeak from 1996-2000, frequently touring with Los Crudos and Catharsis. Currently he is a creative director at Lobo studios, a Manhattan based motion graphics company.

John Porcelly
Youth of Today, Judge, Project X, Shelter, *Schism* fanzine, Schism Records
Known as "Porcell" to his friends, John moved from suburban Connecticut to New York City in the late-1980s where he started *Schism* fanzine and Records with Alex Brown. His bands Youth of Today, Judge, and Project X jump started the second wave of straight edge hardcore and helped spread it globally. John is now a graphic designer and yoga enthusiast, living in Gainesville, Florida and has two beautiful children.

Al Quint
***Suburban Voice* fanzine**
Al continues to produce written and audio dispatches for *Suburban Voice* fanzine/blog and Sonic Overload radio from a secret location in the suburbs of Boston's North Shore. He also writes regular columns for *Maximumrocknroll* and *AMP* magazine.
subvox.blogspot.com
sonicoverload.moocowrecords.com

Larry Ransom
Envy
Larry Ransom is originally from Lockport, New York where he once moshed and stood hard. He is currently living in California and working for professional skateboarder Mike Vallely was well as the comedian Tom Green. In 2008 Larry created Wasted Days TV, which he writes, directs and produces
larryransom.com

Tony Rettman
***Common Sense* fanzine**
Tony went to his first hardcore show at 12, published his own fanzine at 15 and was kicked out of the scene by the age of 21. Since then, Tony has had his writing published in *Thrasher*, *Arthur*, *The Village Voice*, *Swingset*, and *Swindle* as well as regularly contributing to the online fanzines *Blastitude* and *Double Cross*. Rettman had his scene status reinstated sometime in spring of 2006 when he purchased the *Police* 7" by Fucked Up and attended a show by the Boston band Mind Eraser.

ROA
Justice League, Addiction, End to End, Eyelid
ROA began buying every 7" he could afford at Toxic Shock distribution in the early-1980s before singing for Justice League. He currently works in advertising and resides in Los Angeles, California

Shaun Aaron Ross
Excel, *Trendsetter* fanzine
Shaun was born in Los Angeles, California in 1968. He is the son of an Italian immigrant and a Hollywood starlet. In 1985 he founded the band Excel with some of his friends from the Los Angeles graffiti crew KSN (Kings Stop at Nothing). Shaun has worked with: Dogtown, World Industries, Giant Distribution, *Transworld Skateboarding*, *Tokion*, Freshjive, Stussy, U.S.A. Shaolin Temple, Black Panther Party, Bad Brains, Kool Keith, MTV, VH1, E! Networks, and Addict Brand U.K., Currently, Shaun is a high-ranking delegate of the Fuct Love Awareness Program. He is residing and giving thanks in Little Ethiopia, Los Angeles.

Gail Rush
When punk broke in Boston, Gail was at UMass studying photography. She photographed most of the original Boston hardcore bands like SSD, DYS, F.U.'s, Jerry's Kids, and The Freeze, on stage and off. Gail now co-owns New Alliance Audio, a recording studio in Cambridge, Massachusetts with her husband Alvan Long.
newallianceaudio.com

David "Igby" Sattanni
Igby is currently a full-time employee of Revelation Records in Huntington Beach, California. He also runs his own record label, Mankind Records, and still photographs live bands from time to time.

Davo Scheich
Davo started in photography when he was 15 with a 1950s folding camera that he found in his parents attic. The photographs that he saw in *Skateboarder* magazine influenced him to shoot his friends at Endless Summer skatepark, eventually turning his camera on their bands the Necros and Negative Approach. Today, Davo owns a large photo studio specializing in automotive and virtual reality photography. He still skateboards a couple times a week but it's been years since he has been to a punk show.
davo.com

Walter Schreifels
Gorilla Biscuits, Youth of Today, Warzone, Moondog, Quicksand
Walter Schreifels writes and records for various musical projects. In the late 1990s Walter founded Some Records with Sammy Siegler and Matt Pinkus. The name Some Records is a tribute to the now defunct East Village record store of the same name. Walter currently lives in Berlin, Germany.
some.com

Kevin Seconds
7 Seconds, Drop Acid, Positive Force Records
Kevin is originally from Reno, Nevada where he formed the anthemic hardcore band 7 Seconds and started Positive Force Records. He now lives in Sacramento, California where he owns a coffee shop and continues to perform both solo and with 7 Seconds.
kevinseconds.com

Craig Setari
NYC Mayhem, Straight Ahead, Youth of Today, Rest in Pieces, Agnostic Front, Sick of It All
Craig "Ahead" lives in Queens, New York. He currently plays bass for Sick of it All who are still a full time band. When not touring Craig works as a boxing coach.

Robert Shedd
New Jersey native Robert Shedd has worked for Revelation Records and currently runs Collapse Records.

Dave Sine
***Tidbits* fanzine**
David began documenting hardcore shows in the late 1980s for *Tidbits*, a fanzine he published. Dave is married and lives in New Jersey where he still goes to shows, takes lots of photographs, and rides his bicycle many miles.
flickr.com/tidbitsphotos

Dave Smalley
DYS, Down By Law, Dag Nasty, ALL
Dave Smalley was born in California and grew up in Virginia. Dave currently writes songs for a band in his church, and does occasional solo shows. Down By Law has been in semi-hiatus mode, but plans to emerge from the cocoon in the near future.

Joe Snow
Joe was an Anthrax Club regular from 1986 until its demise in 1990. He photographed many of the local bands such as Up Front

and Wide Awake so they had something to use on their records. Joe is an authority of the early Connecticut punk scene which led he and his wife Sue to take the helm of the longstanding Connecticut record label, Incas Records.
incasrecords.com

Erik Lee Snyder
Growing up in Southern New Jersey, Erik discovered hardcore at the age of ten in the form of a Suicidal Tendencies cassette. He is currently living in Brooklyn, New York where he works as a photographer. Erik's photographs have appeared in *Surface* magazine, *ESPN* magazine, and *Entertainment Weekly*.
erikleesnyder.com

Dave Spataro
Dave is a commercial photographer originally from Long Island, New York. He is now married with three children and living in Tampa, Florida.
davespataro.com

Dave Stein
Combined Effort Records
Dave got into hardcore in 1984 and eventually started promoting all-ages VFW hall shows in Albany, New York. He started the record label, Combined Effort and opened the East Village record shop Reconstruction Records, while still in law school. Dave is now a music business lawyer and represents many of the friends he made including Agnostic Front, Sick of It All, Madball and labels with roots in hardcore including Equal Vision and Uprising Records. While his law practice is not exclusive to hardcore, his attitude and approach is.
davestein.com

Sean Taggart
Sean Taggart was raised by hippie artists in New York City. Instead of paying attention in school or trying to find a job, Sean hung out downtown where his friends quickly recognized that he could draw. His iconic illustrations have been seen on the covers of albums by Agnostic Front, The Cro-Mags, Crumbsuckers, and the Jerky Boys, with whom Sean earned a Gold Record.
seantaggart.com

Adam Tanner
Dance of Days fanzine
After years of photographing shows up and down the East Coast, Adam collected his photographs and published *Dance of Days*

fanzine. Since then Adam's photographs have appeared on the cover of Hatebreed's *Satisfaction is the Death of Desire* and in the pages of *Alternative Press, Anti-Matter, All Ages: Reflections on Straight Edge, Rolling Stone, Second Nature, Spin,* and *Skyscraper*.
adamtanner.com

Jeff Terranova
Up Front
Jeff took over Smorgasbord Records in 1996, which he continues to run while also playing bass in Connecticut based band No Image. In May 2001 Jeff started his radio show, The Anti-Emo Empire! on 88.7FM WNHU Thursdays.
up-front.org
smorgasbordrecords.com

Drew Thomas
Bold, Youth of Today, Into Another
Drummer Drew Thomas got his start on the drums at the age of 13 in New York City's hardcore scene, founding Bold and playing on and touring for Youth of Today's *Break Down the Walls* 12". He started seminal post-hardcore outfit Into Another with Richie Birkenhead, recording four albums on Revelation Records and Hollywood Records. He then started New Rising Sons with Garrett Klahn and recorded one album for Virgin Records. He is currently performing with God Fires Man and Bloody Social, both based in New York.
myspace.com/godfiresman
myspace.com/bloodysocial

Ron Vickers
Ron took photographs of several Southern California hardcore bands starting in the late 1980s. He later joined Frosty Crunch from Chain of Strength in the post-hardcore outfit Man Will Surrender who released their self-titled major label debut in 1997.

Brian Walsby
Brian lives in Raleigh North Carolina with his girlfriend and her two children. He currently plays in the band Double Negative and has three of his *Manchild* books out. He recently embarked on a career as a freelance artist and is trying his best to not have to get a real job again. Bug him if you want some crap drawn.
brianwalsby.com

Darren Walters
Hi-Impact Records, Railhed, Jade Tree Records
Darren Walters lives in Wilmington, Delaware where he continues to run the Jade Tree label.

In addition, Darren teaches full-time in the Music Industry program at Drexel University.
jadetree.com

Rich Warwick
Rich sucked at skateboarding and was better at listening to punk and hardcore. He grew up in New Jersey, Washington, D.C., Richmond, Virginia and most importantly Philadelphia. Now residing in Brooklyn, New York he runs the record label Parts Unknown with his non-sexual life partner Jason "Jayskin" Scheller. Rich was a contributing writer to the *Philadelphia Weekly, While You Were Sleeping, Swindle,* and *Restaurant* magazine.

Casey Watson
Casey currently lives in Oakland, California where he is a program supervisor at Thunder Road Adolescent Drug Treatment Center.

Jeff Winterberg
Antioch Arrow
In addition to playing in the highly influential San Diego band Antioch Arrow, Jeff has played in False Island and Coptic Light. He began photographing bands in 1991 and his photos were published in his book *Rat-A-Tat-Tat Birds*. He currently lives in Brooklyn, New York.
jeffwinterberg.com

Lenny Zimkus
Lenny works as an electrician by day, which pays the bills, amateur photographer by night doesn't pay anything. He continues to shoot photos of bands when the mood strikes and is still involved in this scene after 22 years. Lenny is the husband of one, father of two and currently living in New Jersey.
zimkus.com

Christopher Zusi
Release, Ressurection
Chris began going to shows in the mid-1980s in New York City and all over New Jersey where he still resides. He has played guitar in Release, Ressurection, and Floorpunch.

The authors would like to thank the following people for their assistance.
Without them, this project would not have been possible.

Christian Acker, Jerome Albertini, Chris Alpino, Ben Alumbaugh, Ben Alvie, Jackie Anderson, Matt Anderson, Rob Anderson, Peter Amdam, Matthew Ammirati, Robert Arce, Lesley Arfin, Dean Baltulonis, Al Barkley, Luis Barrera, Brett Beach, Justin Beck, Melinda Beck, Julie Benoit, David Bett, Jay Bil, Richie Birkenhead, Jason Bishop, Angela Boatwright, Tom Bolger, Brian Brannon, Norman Brannon, Erik Brunetti, Dave Brown, Shawn Brown, Peter and Sally Brinkerhoff, Malcolm Buick, Katherine Burns, Chris Cannon, Tom Capone, Chris Casali, Curtis Casella, Peter Christofferson, Lollion Chong, Cynthia Connolly, Jordan Cooper, Chris Corry, Mike Courcy, Paul Costuros, Sean Cronan, Chris Daily (Smorgasbord), Geoff D'agostino, Lance Dawes and Independent Trucks, Jeremy Dean, Katherine Deatrick, Justine Demetrick, Vic DiCara, William Dimotta, Tony Donahue, Courtney Dubar, Patrick Dubar, Jared Eberhardt, Kevin Egan, Wes Eisold, John and Rita Elder, Rachel Elder, Jay Ellis, Dana Erickson, Ewan Exalll, Jason Farrell, Eric Ferentz, Jon Field, Matthew Field, James Fitzgerald, Harley Flanagan, Joe D. Foster, Glen E. Friedman, Rick Froberg, Jon Gallagher, Matt Galle, Francesca Gavin, Mark Geist, Damian Genuardi, Mike Gitter, JJ Gonson,Tim Gonzales, Mel Gooch, Jason Gnewikow, Steve Green, Sandro Grison, Ron Guardipee, Jesse Gustafson, Fred Hammer, Tim Harrington, Mike Hartsfield, Karl Hedgepath, Ryan Hoffman, Anna Holloway,

Luke Hoverman, Jacob Hoyc, Russ Iglay, Jordin Isip, Seth Jabour, Sacha Jenkins, Jenny Jensen, Travis Jensen, Casey Jones, Christopher Jones, Jimmy Johnson (Forced Exposure), Brian Jordan, John Joseph, Tonie Joy, Matt Kattman, Justin Thomas Kay, Theresa Kelliher, Tim Kerr, Kelly and TJ Klement, John Knapp, David Koenig, Jason Kristofer, Andrew Kuo, Kevin and Nikki Laing, Rich Labbate, Vernon Laird, Jeff Langlois, John Lacroix, Jay Laughlin, Donna Lee, Sue Lee, Ray Lemoine, Scott Lenhardt, Mark Likosky, Ronny Little, Ian Love, Steve Lowenthal, Megan Lynch, Kevin Lysaght, Ian MacKaye, The Meckler Family, Brian and Melissa Mackin, Charles Maggio, Peter Maher, Dave Mandell, Jamie Manza, Amanda Marsalis, Glenn Maryansky, Robert Mars, Ezra Martin, John Martin, Richard Martin, Steve Martin, Vique Martin, Kent McClard, Craig Metzger, Kimou Meyer, Chris Minicucci, Paul Mittelman, John McLaughlin, Ed McKirdy, John Mcloughlin, Tim and Traci McMahon, Lee Misenheimer, Rusty Moore, Adam Moss, Gibby Miller, Ryan Murphy, Dan Murphy, Dave Murphy, Michael Murphy, Stacey Murray, Adam Nathanson, Dave Natoli, Jeff Nelson, Joe Nelson, Robert Nedorostek, Jeff Neumann, Ted Newsome, Gavin Oglesby, Sean O'Donnell, Ashley Oh, Dan O'Mahony, Jason O'Toole, Michele Outland, Matt Owens, Mark Owens, Tim Owen, BJ Papas, The Pappalardo Family, Ernie Parada, Jacob Pastrovich, Gus Peña, Andy

Perez, Anthony and Traci Persinger, Stefan Petraski, Jason Pettigrew, Artie Phillie, Philin Phlash, Chrissy Piper, Daniel Piwowarczyk, John Porcelly, Mary-Louise Price, Al Quint, Jack Rabid, Todd Ransick, Larry Ransom, Steve Reddy, Sami Reiss, Azy Relph, Tony Rettman, Brian Ristau, ROA, Shaun Ross, Gail Rush, Peter Russo, Ariel Rubio, Mark Ryan, Anthony Saffery, Ken Salerno, Charlotte Salmon, Marissa Santillo, David "Igby" Sattanni, Stephanie Savage, John Scharbach, Davo Scheich, Jason Scheller, Paul Schiek, Ursula JC Schindler, John Stabb Schroeder, Mike Scondotto, Kevin Seconds, Jackie Shapiro, Bob Shedd, Showpaper, Nick Shuit, Sammy Siegler, Trevor Silmser, Mike Simonetti, Dave Sine, Tim Singer, Chris Sleboda, Dave Smalley, Joe and Sue Snow, Erik Lee Snyder, Joseph Songco, Pascal Spengemann, Mark Starr, Christian Stavros, Dave Stein, Karli Stein, Kim Stoerker, Sean Sullivan, Ian Svenonius, Sean Taggart, Adam Tanner, Malcolm Tent, Jeff Terranova, Drew Thomas, Chad Timmreck, Chuck Treece, Chad Timmreck, Ben Treat, Michael Troast, Leslie Twitchell, Fiorella Valdesolo, Mike Vallely, Bart Van Mulders, Rop Vasquez, Ryan Waller, Brian Walsby, Darren Walters, Rich Warwick, David Wasnak, Casey Watson, Chris Weinblad, William Wend, Todd Wender, Eric Weiss, John White, Mark Whiteley, Scott Williams, Jeff Winterberg, Dan Yemin, Lenny Zimkus, Chris Zusi